HCB PUBLISHING

ENERGY

HOW TO UNLEASH YOUR INNER FIRE

CHRIS & KARENE LAMBERT-GORWYN AND DAVID GIL CRISTOBAL

-in collaboration with-

**Lucy Ascham - Kate Gare - Anna Goodwin - Emma Grace
Dr Andrea Haas - Karl Hutchison - Pauline Kirtley
Claudia R Knights - Christine Laidlaw - Jane Mcdowell
Hazel Macfarlane - Lisa Moore - Irma Prins
Simon Rogers - Tara Sutton - Sarah Watt**

ENERGY - HOW TO UNLEASH YOUR INNER FIRE -

ISBN: 978-1-8380061-7-4

Limits of Liability and Disclaimer of Warranty

The author and publisher shall not be liable for your misuse of the enclosed material. This book is strictly for informational and educational purposes only.

Warning – Disclaimer

The purpose of this book is to educate and entertain. The author and/or publisher do not guarantee that anyone following these techniques, suggestions, tips, ideas, or strategies will become successful. The author and/or publisher shall have neither liability nor responsibility to anyone with respect to any loss or damage caused, or alleged to be caused, directly or indirectly by the information contained in this book.

Medical Disclaimer

The medical or health information in this book is provided as an information resource only, and is not to be used or relied on for any diagnostic or treatment purposes. This information is not intended to be patient education, does not create any patient-physician relationship, and should not be used as a substitute for professional diagnosis and treatment.

Publisher

HCB Publishing Ltd.

London

United Kingdom

Printed in EU, UK, Canada and the United States of America

Table of Contents

DEDICATION

To our families, our friends and all the expert authors included in this book.

We love you all and thank you for joining us on the mission of making a difference in this world!

FOREWORD

Powerful Wisdom from leaders in the world of Energy!

Experts are to be admired for their knowledge, but they often remain unrecognised by the general public because they reserve their information and insights for paying customers and clients. There are many experts in any given field, but their impact is limited to the handful of people with whom they work.

This book we hope in part, will change that. It brings together information that would not otherwise be available to the public so that more people can benefit from this expertise. We have specifically chosen experts with a unique experience and story to share so that this information is both accessible, actionable and will support as many people as possible.

Many experts have always dreamed of writing a book to share their expertise and 'superpowers' with the world. Becoming an author however, is a significant undertaking that not everyone turns into a reality. By providing their expertise and contributing to this book, these experts have not only made their dreams a reality, they also offer a much richer experience of life for you, the reader.

We know not everyone has the same experience of Energy and by combining these experts insights and experiences, we hope that you will find yourself in these pages and be able to gain insight, inspiration and perhaps solve your own challenges in this area.

We know that you will learn a lot from reading these chapters and connecting with these experts. Enjoy!

Chris & Karene Lambert-Gorwyn and David Gil Cristobal
Bestselling and Award-Winning Authors

INTRODUCTION

Unlike most books that you might read, this is not a theoretical treaty or fictional discussion of what may or may not work. It is real experience from real people making a real difference that can apply to you own life and circumstances, if you take action.

Bringing together expertise and advice usually reserved for high-paying clients, this book will give you insights, inspiration and most importantly actions so you can make a difference in your life today.

All of the contributing authors have many years of experience, countless successes and of course, a fair few failures. Many of them experienced challenges personally, or had clients or family members who have inspired their journeys and they're now on a mission to share and make solutions, knowledge and experience accessible for more people.

So many people want to make a difference in the world and yet find themselves held back by fear and doubt. The people who have co-authored this book have overcome this to reach more people and make a bigger difference.

If you have picked up this book and have read this far, then you either want to know more or change something in your life. This means that you, like the authors of this book, will have to overcome your fears and doubts.

We know from neuroscience and first-hand experience from training thousands of people, that lasting change requires 3 key elements: the first is KNOWLEDGE, which you will find in these pages; the second is your MINDSET, which again this book will influence; and lastly a supportive COMMUNITY.

We hope you will find this community in the stories and experiences included in these pages. By their sharing their own experiences and the stories of those they have treated, supported and made a difference for, the authors will provide you with an all-important community of support for you to move forward.

You may recognise yourself or others in these pages and we hope that will inspire you to take action and make a difference. By stepping into our best selves and living our best life, we become the change we want to see in the world. Whilst we might feel insignificant as individuals, our collective powers are boundless, so keep reading and see what differences you might be able to create for you, your life, family and those around you.

Chris & Karene Lambert-Gorwyn and David Gil Cristobal
Bestselling and Award Winning Authors

ENERGY

Energy is that special ingredient that makes everything else work better. If you had more energy, you'd be able to do more, concentrate for longer, work harder, live more. Very simply, having more energy means everything becomes easier and success in every area of life becomes more likely.

Energy is the under-appreciated magic that makes or breaks everything else in life. When we have it, we feel great and everything is possible. When we don't have it, life is hard and everything becomes more challenging.

And yet, increasing our energy levels, like losing weight, is actually very simple. Whilst there are entire mountains of science and research into how energy works and ways we can increase our energy levels, fundamentally we all forget how simple it really is...

"Do more of what gives you energy and less of what depletes it"

It isn't any more complicated than this, yet, like so many things in life, it's almost like we can't believe it could be this simple.

So what will give you energy?

The list is endless and includes the obvious, such as sleep, healthy food, exercise, breathing, and meditation; as well as the less obvious and less scientifically recognised, such as laughter, friendship, spiritual connection, living with purpose, and love.

And what will deplete it?

Sometimes our energy is depleted by the simple absence of things that give us energy such as a lack of sleep or not eating healthy food. However, there are also specific things that deplete our energy levels in overt and/or covert ways, such as negative thought patterns, gossip-style or negative conversations, financial concerns and money worries, fear, unhappy romantic relationships, incomplete tasks, overwhelm or boredom.

“Do more of what gives you energy and less of what depletes it”

Personally, I know only too well what it’s like to have no energy. Not just low energy where you feel a bit run-down, or struggle to get up in the morning; but the complete absence of energy so your mind and body feels completely shut down. So much so that even a single flight of stairs would leave me gasping and having to sit down to recover; and a simple 5 minute conversation would be a huge mental challenge leaving me exhausted with my brain struggling to keep up with what was being said.

I struggled with Chronic Fatigue Syndrome, also known as CFS or ME, for several years and was unable to work, sometimes unable to even get out of bed for much of that time. Life became a constant battle of trying to preserve and build my energy so I could complete even the most simple of activities.

I tried anything and everything to restore my energy levels with mixed success. However, over several years, I slowly grew to learn the simple truth: when I simply did more of what gave me energy each day and less of what depleted it, I made progress. It wasn’t consistent and didn't always follow a clear pattern but as long as each day I did more things that boosted my energy, slowly and progressively over months and years, I recovered.

Trying to continue living my life the way it was before getting sick and just trying to push through the 'weakness' didn't work. Then again, neither did just resigning myself to being sick and having no energy. Instead, the daily focus on what built energy and a daily awareness of what depleted it, had the biggest impact over time.

The startling thing I discovered was that it wasn't always the obvious things that made the biggest difference.

For example,

Negative Conversations:

I started to notice that some of my friends had a very negative outlook on life and every conversation with them left me drained. Once I recognised this, I consciously chose to limit my interactions with these friends and started spending more time in conversations and with people who had a more positive outlook on life.

Filling my mind:

Paying attention to what I filled my mind with each day, such as the books I read, the movies and TV I watched. I noticed the more I filled my mind with things that inspired me or made me curious, or caused me to laugh, the better I felt.

Toxic Relationships:

Recognising and finally admitting to myself how

dysfunctional and traumatic my first marriage was and that we had to separate and get divorced for both of our sakes. Whilst the break-up and ensuing divorce was very painful and stressful, it also removed a huge drain on my energy levels as I was finally being true to myself and my own feelings. The self-awareness that came from this paved the way for the fulfilling and supportive relationship I now treasure with my wife Karene.

Having Purpose & finding Fulfilment:

Coming to terms with what I loved about my work and also what I hated about it allowed me to identify what I needed long term. Getting up each morning with drive and purpose compared with dreading the day to come, is like night and day in terms of energy levels. As I progressively did more and more of what made my eyes 'shine' my energy levels expanded equally.

Laughing:

Children laugh more than adults. And they have a LOT more energy. There's an obvious connection and fortunately science is just now catching up and proving that laughter has a host of benefits such as improving our immune systems, increasing cognitive alertness, improving facial muscle tone and increasing our general sense of well-being, including our energy levels.

Personally, I started noticing that days when I laughed, I felt better and had more energy.

So I made a point to laugh more. Sounds pretty simplistic but then the best solutions often are.

"Do more of what gives you energy and less of what

depletes it"

This simple concept allowed me to transform my life. Could it do the same for you?

This book is filled with many more suggestions and strategies of how to transform your energy levels. The Experts gathered in these pages are some of the best there are at helping people re-ignite their energy levels. Put their knowledge, their experience and their expertise to work in your life and discover what might be possible for you. Life is too short to just suffer through and there are too many things awaiting your greatness for you to just sit back saying, "I'm too tired". Use this book and the expert knowledge within these pages to get the energy and motivation for life that you've always dreamed of!

Wishing you every success!

Chris Lambert-Gorwyn

chris@heartcentredbusiness.com

I Grow Heart Centred Businesses from Passion to Profit

Lucy Ascham

Lucy Ascham has nearly two decades of teaching individuals and facilitation practice, with 1000s of clients, 100s of workshops and seminars. She is based in Sheffield UK and works online worldwide.

She teaches and facilitates women to become empowered leaders in their own lives, returning them from pain and suffering into the noble force of nature they are. She enables people to find harmony and peace in any situation. "We don't choose our fate, but we can use it to our best advantage by choosing our response and restoring freedom".

Lucy helps women become more energized, empowered and effective.

She advocates learning to say "Yes" to your one precious Life.

Website: www.lucyascham.com

Email: lucy@lucyascham.com

Phone: +44 7949 522 655

Facebook: Lucy Ascham With Poise

What If Raising Your Energy Is About Doing Less?

What if raising your energy is about doing less, aligning yourself to the truth and natural order?

What if you could see a body and soul plumber to help unblock your energy and get it flowing more freely?

Would you be interested to learn more?

At the heart of what I do is a simple idea, that we can restore health and vitality by rebalancing our system. There are many layers of systems – your body, family, community, country and so on. I look at symptoms, people and circumstances as part of the widest system and help make repairs and connections for the greatest flow of love and life. By supporting people to work systemically, symptoms can be healed and difficulties transformed.

When I work with people experiencing relationship difficulties, physical ailments, the effects of surgery, traumatic life events etc., I am looking at what is blocking the flow and taking steps to unblock that. When we see and agree to the truth of what is there, we stop resisting the facts of our one precious life and we stop wasting energy.

I work with principles found in nature – body and soul movements. I help people consciously cooperate with 'what is' and restore their alignment with the natural order of their unique system.

Think of a garden hose which has various squashed parts; obviously the water doesn't flow so well. I see people's energy blocked in kinks and knots from various life experiences and I can help them become more free and disentangled, so that their life energy flows forward in the best way possible.

A good resolution through working with me might include relief from symptoms, unhealthy behaviours, addictions or finding peace with a difficult fate.

It is mainly women who come to me with long-standing problems that no talking therapy or treatment seems to touch. Their issues are deeply personal, emotional and physical which blocks them leading the life they want to live. Somehow even after much self-development work, they are still stuck. Often it takes a crisis for them to come for healing support.

That's where I come in. I give people the opportunity to clear the real reasons behind why they might be stuck so that they can move on. Some of these reasons may be known, a practical reason for stuck energy, whereas, at other times we need to look deeper, wider and further back: our family's history can help unlock some secrets and mysteries.

Annabel had online sessions presenting with persistent neck pain, after breast surgery from cancer. She said she felt strangled and remembered the way her grandfather died. I helped her see the unconscious patterns and entanglements, to release them with love. "Lucy's sessions were amazing. Her unique blend of skills helped me have good posture without effort. Before this I had seen many physiotherapists and osteopaths but the pain kept coming back within a few weeks. Within my first session with Lucy the difference was so clear that my friends commented on it."

My way of understanding health is that symptoms can actually be Life pointing out how we are literally out-of-order; the pain alerts us to deeper undercurrents and issues.

Using the body system for example, we can be strengthened by resting, by finding the right order for everyday movements and by using our muscle tone appropriately. We are mammals and our coordination lies in the free relationship between the head and the spinal column. I see the spine as our core, like an apple core, which runs along our vertical axis. When this relationship works well, our postural muscles support our torso - and then reaching, carrying and locomotion.

One thing I do is teach people how to really rest – not just switch off and slump in front of a screen. When we consciously and constructively rest we allow the whole system to be reunited – body, mind and emotions so we can move and live more easily, with more motivation, stamina and choice.

Do you know that our brain copes with shock and traumas by wrapping up the energy of these events and storing the memory in our body until we have more resources to unpack and integrate them? We go into survival mode so we can do what we need to do in the short term - and life somehow carries on. It goes on, in some version as we get used to less zest for life and get pulled down by the hidden weight of events while the real reasons get muffled and held with unconscious muscle tension.

Sometimes the deeper reason why you are in pain is not illness or injury but how you move, the way you walk, the way you hold your head when you talk or stand - mostly on one leg with arms crossed – all these habits can put strain on your back, your core. It requires effort to stay off-balance. Add some unconscious tension and trauma and things can easily go askew. Unconsciously most people are wasting energy, in many small and damaging ways. It is possible to stop this energy leak and habitual eroding of joints and freedom. Working together with new knowledge, changing mind and muscle patterns we can restore order within ourselves for our best health. Good coordination is fundamental to every movement.

Emotional traumas can come from huge life experiences – accidents, sudden or early deaths, war, migration – the weight of these is often too much for one person to bear. When we bring the systemic lens to the situation, to their body or family, we release the deeper forces at work – and love and ease can flow more readily.

We may tell ourselves that we 'should be over it by now' as the event happened years ago. 'That trauma happened when I was a child or teenager it can't still be bothering me.' And yet it is. It is lying dormant in our system and may come out later in aches, pains and illness or unhealthy behaviours. The blockage may even come from previous generations and still be playing out today. I help people re-balance their own body-mind-soul system for themselves and for the benefit of their wider system too.

Martha came to me hoping to improve her self-esteem and family relationships which were a sore subject to them after childhood trauma. With my help she began to see larger factors contributing to the dynamics in her family and what their impact has been on the individuals involved.

She said "It is as though I have been gifted an entirely new lens through which to view human behaviour, and it is a lens of compassion and empathy like no other. Due to this, I have been able to come to terms with the way my family operates, which has proven to be a great relief. I would definitely recommend working with Lucy. She held such a safe space for me and my vulnerability with great compassion and authenticity."

The issue she struggled with didn't start with her. Saying 'Yes' to what is true and unchangeable can be an energy lift in itself. I helped her take responsibility for her share of what happened, release the rest and so free up her energy for her best life.

For two decades I have been working with people to help relieve their tension patterns, suffering and help get them back in charge of their life and get their energy moving more freely again.

I see myself as a body and soul plumber. I am looking for what blocks the natural flow of energy, movement and aliveness. The modalities I work with are like streams coming into a mature river with power to help bring movement and healing to seemingly intransigent issues.

To get your energy moving more efficiently so love and life can flow more freely, call Lucy on 07949 522 655.

Kate Gare

Empowering others to live powerful lives since 2007

Speaker, Coach, Therapist, Trainer

Founder of The Live Powerfully Programme. I support high achieving women from all over the world who balance everything but are feeling less joy, more tired and more 'is this it?'. I help them get rid of the stuff they don't need and build more of what they do so they get their zest back and thrive no matter what happens.

One of the world's most experienced Lightning Process ™ Practitioners – applying the science of the mind-body connection to re-build health.

Website: www.everylife.com

Email: kate@everylife.com

Phone: +44 (0)7964 844375

Instragram: @katelivingpowerfully

Facebook: https://www.facebook.com/everylife.LivePowerfully/

LinkedIn: https://www.linkedin.com/in/kate-gare/

What If You Are The Key To Unlocking Abundant Energy?

Do you feel constantly tired? Are you overwhelmed by a lack of work-life balance? Would you like more vivacity to live the life you want?

Stress and pressure are so pervasive in modern life that we barely register the damage to our health. In fact, our unmanageable workloads are viewed as a sign of success, a 'badge of honour' that validates us to our partners, friends, and colleagues.

But these damaging perceptions hold us back from leading a fulfilling life and we should not feel like a failure if we need support. Pushing through a whirlwind of obligations zaps our physical, mental and emotional energy and we become trapped in a cycle of stress and exhaustion. We ignore the 'nudges' that we need to make a drastic change.

As the creator of the *Live Powerfully Programme* and an advanced Lightning Process practitioner, I believe people should not have to reach burnout or be suffering from chronic health conditions before they seek support. We have a choice when we acknowledge that 'enough is enough' and we deserve to discover how to thrive at life.

Since 2007, I have supported more than 1,000 high-achieving women from all over the world who are balancing their lives but are finding it harder to perform, feeling energy depleted and are not living a life they love.

The *Live Powerfully Programme* draws on principals from the mind-body connection, positive psychology, neuroscience and the neurobiology of stress. Clients are guided to break down barriers to success including their own limiting self-beliefs, in order to build and embrace their personal power. This is achieved by taking charge of their personal and professional lives, making choices that lead to fulfilment and nurturing a joyful and optimistic relationship with their sense of self for good.

Clients of mine, who previously struggled with debilitating stress and became overwhelmed, are now conquering mountains! They have introduced powerful new routines into their everyday life, and their practice has become second nature.

As a coach, therapist and trainer, I understand the challenges my clients face such as fatigue and trauma also shaped my own personal and professional journey:

> I first experienced severe ill health in my mid-twenties. I was on track with my career, but I was placing huge pressure on myself to excel at all costs. I ignored the warning signs until I became sick with a virus. Days blurred into weeks as I did not recover, and I became practically bed bound by severe headaches, fatigue, a foggy brain and joint pain.
>
> Over seven years, I spent thousands of pounds on treatments, but nothing helped. Then I discovered The Lightning Process ™. I was instantly inspired by the energy between the mind and the body,

and understood how its connection was the key to getting my life back.

I had already trained as a practitioner when I met my husband, Stuart. We began trying for a family and fell pregnant via IVF. But an undiagnosed heart condition resulted in heart failure and spontaneous labour at 31 weeks. Our premature twins, Harry and Edie, arrived via emergency caesarean and needed intensive care to survive.

Six weeks later, Harry and Edie came home. The traumatic birth, the anxious weeks of watching our babies struggle...these experiences became a blur as life became incredibly busy. I went back to work, we took on a house refurbishment and I had several operations. Sure enough, I became overwhelmed and I needed to create space to process everything that had happened to flourish again. I recognised I needed to replenish my energy and resilience to strengthen a sustainable, happier life for myself and my family – not just for the next few months, but as part of a healthy, daily practice.

For the last five years, I have continued to refine The Live Powerfully Programme. I believe passionately in helping others and that we all have the capacity to influence our health and key to this is our personal energy. From my extensive experience, it is really important we do not ignore the following 'nudges' as signs from our body that something is not right:

- **CONSTANT FATIGUE:** Are you always tired, even after sleep? Do you crave a holiday, yet find that a vacation is not enough to help your exhaustion? It is impossible to perform at your best if you are permanently fatigued.

- **FEELING FREQUENTLY OVERWHELMED:** Are you spinning so many plates that just one more will bring your world crashing down? Do you feel ineffective and in fear of failure, no matter how hard you work? These feelings of being overwhelmed drain your time and energy and can lead to anxiety and physical stress, such as muscle pain and headaches.
- **INABILITY TO CONCENTRATE:** Is your mind too scattered to enjoy a book or a film? When our brains are stressed and tired, it is difficult to focus. And if we lose the ability to immerse ourselves in the things we love, our self-care dissipates, we feel less joy and we begin to cope rather than succeed at life.

Sound familiar? I support my clients to address the imbalances and rebalances in their lives.

Imagine you are rowing down a river full of rocks and reeds. As you navigate your way downstream, you are repeatedly snagged and bumped, losing an oar and damaging your boat. But what happens if you raise the water levels high enough to glide easily over the rocks and reeds? The obstacles no longer register on your journey.[1]

This metaphor illustrates how we use resilience to boost our mental and physical energy, to deal with tougher times. If the rocks and reeds represent challenges and the water our energy and resilience, we need to work out what 'drains' the river and what increases the water level. Energy and resilience are like physical

1 Metaphor from Professor Patrick Pietroni, (www.huffpost.com/author/patrick-pietroni) a leading authority in mental health and resilience in the UK

fitness. You train to get stronger– there is no quick fix and it takes commitment and focus to maintain it. I encourage my clients to start nurturing their power to find their zest for life by practicing the following:

- **DO MORE OF WHAT MAKES YOU HAPPY:** Can you think back when you last felt 100% pure contentment? Did you truly acknowledge and value it? Believe that you deserve to prioritise time doing what brings you joy. Exercise, connection with others or learning a new skill... these experiences raise our resilience and ability to bounce back with energy after challenging times.
- **BE KIND TO YOURSELF:** The key to living powerfully is our relationship with ourselves. Our beliefs, identity, actions and behaviours feed into our energy and validity. It is estimated we have between 50,000 and 70,000 thoughts a day[1], so drop any negative self-talk and treat yourself with compassion. Change your self-beliefs, e.g. "I'm not good enough" and be kind to yourself to nurture high self-esteem and watch internal conflict transform into abundant energy.
- **PRIORITISE PROPER REST AND RELAXATION:** A regular circadian rhythm is vital if you want to produce healthy brain chemicals such as Serotonin (mood and pleasure) and Dopamine (motivation and stress tolerance). Sleep has been shown to protect the mitochondria, the powerhouse of your cells. A sleep routine is a good starting point but stressing about achieving a full eight hours is counterproductive. Take the pressure off and aim for calm and peaceful rest throughout the night, using a breathing practice

to help you before tackling bigger issues.

Because of the success my clients have experienced, I know the Live Powerfully Programme enables people to take control and thrive at work and home, no matter what happens. Let me guide you on your journey to wellbeing and fulfilment. And why not? We are all guilty of putting ourselves at the bottom of the priority pile, but we would always want positive change for our loved ones. So be kind to yourself. Starting now, choose to believe you deserve this opportunity.

I will support you and you will make change.

Change your life today by booking a FREE discovery call with Kate Gare and as a BONUS receive her popular '5 Keys To Unlocking Your Personal Resilience' e-book by quoting 'Energy'. Call, email or book directly https://BookNow-KateGare.as.me/DiscoveryCall

Credentials and Qualifications:

- Kate Gare BA (Hons) Dip Clin Hyp NLP
- Founder of The Live Powerfully Programme
- Resilience Practitioner
- Heath Math Coach
- Life Coach
- Clinical Hypnotherapist
- NLP Practitioner
- Advanced Lightning Process ™ Practitioner

Anna Goodwin

Managing Director of Heart Centred Business

Anna Goodwin excels at helping people get out of their own way, so that they can get unstuck in their lives and businesses. Mumpreneur and Managing Director at Heart Centred Business, Anna trains experts how to make a bigger difference in the world and get paid what they're truly worth.

A former Secondary School teacher who left teaching to set up her own successful enterprise, Anna helped hundreds of women overcome anger and regain a spring in their step. Watching the women she supported regain their passion for life and step into their true potential led Anna to bring her expertise to the award-winning company Heart Centred Business in the role of Managing Director. With clients typically achieving £50,000-£100,000 growth within 12 months of implementing their systems, Anna and the Heart Centred Business team support women to create an income, a business and a mindset beyond anything they believed to be possible.

Anna Goodwin

Website: www.heartcentredbusiness.com

Email: anna@heartcentredbusiness.com

Phone: +44 (0)333 987 4245

Are You A Business Owner And Have You Lost Your Mojo?

If you are, it might be that you have one (or more) of the most frequent complaints - lack of time, lack of money or lack of clients. Either way, if you don't know what you are doing in the right order and at the right time it may leave you feeling like you are alone and lacking in motivation and energy. If this is you, I get it!

I'm Anna Goodwin, the Managing Director at Heart Centred Business, where we train experts how to make a bigger difference in the world and how to turn their passion into profit.

Having worked with thousands of practitioner businesses over the last 8 years - we know that there are three key steps to creating the energy we need to stay in 'motivated' action:

Step 1) Knowledge, because we need to do the right things in the right order.

Step 2) Mindset - because when we change this, it makes implementing the knowledge so much simpler and more effective.

Step 3) Community - which acts a bit like the glue. Bringing the mindset and knowledge together by supporting each other in similar goals, similar values, similar actions and most importantly coming together to inspire and generate energy! Sounds good? Yes... it really is!

In this chapter I am going to talk about the power of community and how this impacts our energy to be in action; because without action - nothing changes!

Even though it seems like a life time away, it's only 8 years since I embarked on setting up my own practitioner business. I had a ton of enthusiasm, some amazing skills under my belt and a wish to help others. I worked long hours and had a good go at doing what I thought would work. Unfortunately, those first four years of 'trying' super hard did not provide the results I was looking for! Looking back, I just didn't know what to do, when to do it and I had no-one around me who had done it successfully before. Needless to say when you are working hard, going around in circles, it impacts even the most positive of people. Not only did I seriously lose my mojo for action but my confidence and my energy levels took a hit across the board.

Feeling in a massive flunk and close to throwing the towel in - I found myself in a room with 50 other practitioner businesses on a 3 day training; teaching us the blue-print of how to earn 6 figures from our passion. In amongst this new community the 'ah-ha' moments came thick and fast. I resonated with the theory behind the systems and mindset changes, however, what I found most curious was abundance of energy and enthusiasm from the trainers and the team. It was this infectious energy that sparked a fire in me and joining a community filled with tonnes of energy became my saving grace.

I would love to say that the next bit of the journey was easy - it wasn't. I had no idea I had ground to such a halt in the last few years, and it took a massive effort to get started and then keep the momentum going. I felt like a butterfly breaking out of its chrysalis - my body and mind pushing and pulling with every new action I was taking. It turned out I had many fears that stood in my way - and my default was to crawl under the covers and go to sleep. To move forward, sometimes I did the internal mind work, other times I burst my way through - in a 'fake it 'til you make it' type way. Finding the energy to take actions was most certainly the biggest challenge. There is no way I would have been able to keep going without a community keeping my fire burning and consistently re-setting my energy and motivation.

I had a community that saw me much bigger than I knew myself to be: Bigger than my excuses. Bigger than my massive flunk... and they loved me enough to tell me what I needed to hear, rather than what I wanted! I love the quote 'Change The Way You Look At Things And The Things You Look At Change' (Wayne Dyer). When they helped me change the way I saw the world; yes, my intentions and actions shifted but maybe more importantly I started to wake up! Those first few months were certainly a struggle, but once the wheel of energy (and momentum) was turning - I was off!

My energy was now 100% improved but it was not consistent enough yet. I was going from strength to strength in terms of energy and my actions, which reflected in my results! I was also now seeing what might be possible if I could just take it all up another gear. Jim Rohn said that 'we are the average of the five people we spend the most time with'; with this in mind, I decided to spend any and every opportunity I could with the team - as a helper or as a student - you name it, I was there. It worked every time: Yes, I always grew massively in those moments but it provided the energy boost and motivation I needed to spur me on to the next mini milestone.

Over the following 4 years, I grew my business exponentially before being offered the incredible opportunity of becoming the Managing Director of Heart Centred Business. I now have the privilege of supporting our current community of more than 200 other practitioner business owners on a similar journey. Everyone has their own peaks and troughs - but the one thing that stands out always for me, is the change in energy when we are together as a powerful community: It does so much more than offer support, love and guidance. When we grow our energy together as a community - it reshapes how we learn, how we take actions, how we show up in the world and alters our mindsets around what's possible.

I am still exploring how to manage and generate more energy, and I am happy I can now tell the difference between being low in energy because of lifestyle, compared with just being fearful about taking an action. There is always more to learn, and the community is more important than ever... but rather than wanting to hide under the covers, growth and new actions now feel exciting! I thank my lucky stars every day that I got to wake up!

If my story resonates with you, do go now and find yourself a community, it will be the best thing you ever did. As Albert Einstein said, 'The definition of insanity is doing the same thing over and over again, but expecting different results.' So make sure your community is one that dishes out a healthy serving of 'tough love', to encourage a different energy, that leads to different actions, that generates different outcomes. If you are curious about the community I have been sharing - great! Please do be in contact, I would love to explore what might be possible for you too.

There are several options to move you forward now:

- If you are in the business of helping others - I am happy to offer you a free strategy call now to help your business move forward. www.heartcentredbusiness.com/free-strat-call
- If you want to start a business journey, where you help more people and make more money. Go now to - 'Find your Passion and Earn your first £1000' - www.passiontoprofitforpractitioners.com/first-1000

* Or go and buy the amazing, bestselling 'Grow Your Heart Centred Business' book from www.heartcentredbusiness.com/book. 358 pages of doing the right things in the right order. This is not a book on theory - but one written from real experience growing thousands of businesses and it will get you taking the right actions to grow your passion or business fast!

Emma Grace

Emma Grace specialises in helping professional women in their 40s who are usually passionate and enthusiastic, but find life is feeling a bit "bleugh". Their body aches, work is tedious, and their relationships jangle – and they're frustrated because they know life can be so much better. Emma helps them feel younger than they have in years, excited and inspired at work, and happy in their relationships, so their lives are transformed in ways they couldn't have imagined. They go from "bleugh" to "WOOHOO!!!".

Diagnosed with a serious illness at 22, following a mere bout of 'flu, Emma was told by doctors that she would probably spend the rest of her life in bed. The illness took her whole life with it, but Emma was determined her future would be better. So she threw herself into learning everything she could about health and wellbeing. She slowly, slowly, learnt her way back to health. It took 10 years.

Starting from scratch in her early 30s, Emma was well but life was a bit...bleugh. She kept looking, studying and successfully working with many clients with challenges in life and health. It took a long time...but she found her WOOHOO!!! Combining decades of experience to create her own system, Emma's clients now get the sort of journey to WOOHOO that she wishes hers had been.

Emma's driving belief is that each human being is unique and infinitely precious. The world needs the special thing that they bring, and they deserve to be the best of themselves – and well – and happy. WOOHOO!!!

Email: emmagracetherapy@gmail.com

Phone: +44(0)7392 079 646

Doing All The Right Things But You're Still Tired?

Here's the secret. Prepare to be surprised...

You eat well. You sleep well. You keep fit. You know how to look after yourself. So why are you still tired?

I was told I would be bed-bound for the rest of my life. Now I am running two businesses and living my busy, happy, dancing life in London, helping amazing people get out of pain, get more energy, and transform their lives. Would you like to know the secret?

It was a long and surprising journey for me. Just turned 22, I was so weak that even breathing was a battle. Following nothing more remarkable than flu, I had been told that I would probably be like that for the rest of my life, and there was nothing they could do to help. I'm an independent, sociable, ambitious woman, and – well, would you accept a future of daytime TV, no friends, no work, and no hope? It took 10 years of fighting and experimenting and being treated by some of the best people I have ever met to get better. The key to that was so unexpected, it took me years to get my head around. Since then, I've worked with hundreds of people in pain and distress, developing my unique method for helping people be well and happy. There are as many ways to help as there are people, but there is that one thing that always, without fail, makes the difference between wellness and illness, energy and exhaustion.

Are you bold enough?

Let me tell you about my client Steven. Steven had too much on to have fun. He had started a new job – a big step up, there were big demands and big rewards, it was the achievement of a lifetime. He was working incredibly long hours to prove himself. And then his sister left her abusive marriage, and she and her son came to stay with him. Steven threw himself into supporting them, desperate to keep them safe and help them start to heal.

Steven started to find he was so tired he was falling asleep in meetings, yet he couldn't sleep at night. He could hardly think straight. He started getting terrible pain in his back. There was certainly no enjoyment in life – everything was a grind. But what could he do? There was no way he would step back from his family. Could he really risk the job he'd worked all his life to achieve? There was literally nothing that could give. But his health was giving, and so was his ability to step up for his job or his sister.

That was the thing: his health, his body were telling him something. Steven had been powering through, but he had gone beyond his limits, and his brain and body were starting to shut him down. It's a survival technique of our subconscious brain: we break, so we don't die. These early signs – these were friendly messengers. I am not going to repeat the name Steven gave them. But friendly they are, and although he resisted, when his stomach started to act up too, he finally accepted something had to be done.

What can you do when everything is necessary and

nothing can give? What Steven needed was to change how he was functioning in body, mind, and life, which meant reducing the stress and increasing the feel-good chemicals. How? Steven needed to do stuff that made him feel good. But he had no time!

Slowly we worked out how it could be done. Comedy podcasts on the way to work. Three minutes between meetings listening to one of his favourite songs. Ten push-ups in a quiet hallway on his way back from the loo. He loved making models, so cleared 20 minutes before bed to do that – and slept so much better for the head space. He really, really wanted to run but there was no time. So he was bold and ruthless, and decided that two lunchtimes a week, no matter what, he would take half an hour and have a run. That was a tough call against all the other demands on his time. But he did it.

And he found that he started to be able to cope again. Small actions. Huge results. The friendly messengers let Steven know he'd hit a wall. He listened, made the tough call to make some changes, and was determined in creating those small spaces. He did things he loved. It gave him the resources he needed to function. And he was able to show up completely to support his sister and nephew, and got stunning results in his job. He also met someone special, but that's another story...

Are you listening? *Really* listening?

Does this seem obvious to you? Do you already look after yourself? So did Jennifer. She had a high-powered career in finance for 25 years, but wanted to embrace her gift for jewellery making, and build her own business. As you know, career changes take time, so Jennifer found herself working in two demanding fields, but she took good care of her health: ate well, slept well, exercised, found time for herself. Did all the right things. She had been on top of it.

And then suddenly, she wasn't. She was exhausted. Everything felt like a chore. It was all just bleugh. Jennifer assumed this was due to a really busy time she'd had, and took a week off. But she rested. And rested. And still felt so exhausted she could barely move, barely leave the house, and still everything felt bleugh. She just assumed she had been more tired than she realised – but I suspected there was something else going on. Jennifer's father lived abroad, and he was very elderly and frail. Jennifer was worried about his health, and worried she may never see him again. And the prospect of his passing also brought up tensions with her sister, and the old family patterns from which she had tried to free herself.

Jennifer had been ignoring these feelings. They felt too much to deal with. And she had other stuff she needed to focus on.

But the friendly messengers were raising their flags. Jennifer agreed to take another weekend for herself. Switch everything off. And then really nurture herself – fill the time with all the things that made her feel good, calm, safe. Re-read her favourite book, wrapped in her favourite rug, with tea in her favourite mug. Eat meals that made her feel nurtured. Spend time in her garden in the sun. Although a passionate runner, she didn't have the energy for that, so she went for a walk to her local park and sat there, overlooking the lake she likes to run round, reconnecting with the place she loves. And taking quiet time and space for reflection.

Jennifer emerged from the weekend with incredible

clarity. She had found the peace, space, and inner safety to hear what she needed to hear. Although she had initially rejected the idea, she knew she had to see a counsellor to deal with those deep family feelings. She realised she wasn't doing enough on her new business, which was her passion, so decided to dial down the work she was doing on financial contracts.

Have you experienced the power of hearing what's going on for yourself and deciding to act on it? These small changes helped Jennifer to come to peace with her past and to shape her future. Spotting the problems and deciding to act on them gave her the energy she needed to take the actions. She listened to the friendly messengers until she heard them, and acted. Her energy flooded back. And she is stepping into her full, glorious potential, and living her passion.

If you want to learn how your body and mind can help you massively increase your energy so you can step into the life you really wish you could live, get in touch with Emma for a free Coaching Session on 07392 079 646, emmagracetherapy@gmail.com.

Dr Andrea Haas

Health Happiness and Inner Strength

Surrey's holistic, medication-free approach to facial pain

With over 30 yrs experience of working as a musculoskeletal doctor on the NHS, including working at the Royal London Hospital for Integrated Medicine, in private practice and for the army, Andrea has a wealth of experience. More recently this has led her into working in Pain Management.

Over the last 15 years she has become more interested in the mind and its impact on the body. 10 yrs ago she branched out as a therapist realising that she could offer her clients so much more this way. Using a variety of tools, often described as a toolbox, Andrea works in a holistic way, helping her clients move forward, not just with their pain, but also in other areas of their lives.

Website: www.andrea-inner-strength.co.uk

Email: andrea@andrea-inner-strength.co.uk

Phone: +447770 672122

Has It Ever Occurred To You That Your Energy Levels May Be Affected By Your Mindset?

We all know that a bad night's sleep, a stressful job or being ill can reduce our energy levels, but our mindset can too. Have you ever wondered why some days, such as the weekend, it is so much easier to get up in the mornings than during the week? Or perhaps you have a great idea, but when it comes to the crunch, you just can't find the energy to start it? Or maybe you're someone who throws yourself into a project for a few days or weeks, then suddenly you lose energy and the job never gets completed. Well, your mindset has a lot to do with all these scenarios and it can be improved by some simple strategies.

I am Dr Andrea Haas and I love working with professional, health conscious women aged between 45 and 55 who suffer with persistent facial pain. So why, I hear you ask, am I writing about energy? Well, a lot of my clients suffer with a lack of energy due to their pain. Pain not only affects their sleep, but also causes frustration or despondency. This demotivates them, in other words affects their mindset. Whether you suffer from a lack of energy due to persistent pain or due to another reason, how to deal with it is the same. So, what do I mean by mindset?

Your mindset is all about how you perceive a situation, the thoughts and feelings, emotions and beliefs around it. We all see the world from different viewpoints depending on the experiences we have had in the past. A good analogy is of two journalists being asked to report on a specific event, and they both report something different. Let's say there was a large building on fire, and most of the fire was at the front of the building. The journalist standing at the front would see, and therefore report, something very different to the journalist who was standing at the back of the building where the fire couldn't be seen, yet they both attended the same scene. This is the same reason why, when there has been a challenging event within a family, maybe an illness or bereavement, the family members all react in different ways even though they have experienced the same event. And what has made them experience it differently is their thoughts and beliefs around the event. What are the emotions around lack of energy?

Feeling demotivated, lazy or bored are ways in which lack of energy can show itself. But if we can turn these emotions around to things like excitement, curiosity and fun and find a reason for completing the action, suddenly we feel motivated. This is the reason why we are able to get up in the middle of the night full of energy to catch a flight for a 2 week holiday somewhere in the sun.

A few years ago I decided to redecorate the kitchen. It was looking shabby and dull. I made a list of what I needed, went down to the local DIY shop and bought everything. But when it came to start, standing in my kitchen and staring at everything that needed to be done, it all suddenly seemed like a mammoth job. I felt overwhelmed and rooted to the spot. I just couldn't find the energy; I didn't know where to start. But I had committed myself now. I also knew that it would look so much better when done. But how was I going to motivate myself?

I came up with a plan. I listed all the positive reasons why the kitchen needed to be decorated. It would look much cleaner, brighter and fresher. I would enjoy being in my kitchen much more. I imagined in my mind's eye how the kitchen would look once it was finished. I also imagined how I would feel when it was completed. I would feel a sense of accomplishment, satisfaction and pride.

I then worked out in what order I was going to do things. I broke the job down into main tasks – sanding woodwork, rubbing down walls, masking tape, painting walls, painting woodwork. Each task was broken down further into smaller tasks. I then knew exactly where I was going to start and what the next step was. This stopped me wasting energy at each step working out what I was going to do next. I also planned how much time I could realistically put aside each day and on which days of the week. Would I be able to do a morning a week for 10 days, or did I only have the weekends? This then gave me a time scale to accomplish it in.

Each day I gave myself a task to complete, telling myself I could then reward myself by reading my book or having a coffee or ringing a friend. What I found was that the task I completed then moved on to another task, which moved on to another, and before I knew it, I had completed far more tasks than planned. The reward had been forgotten about because there was a feeling of accomplishment. This is how I progressed, and the kitchen got completed in record time. I found by giving myself bite size chunks of jobs which seemed manageable with the potential of a reward, and doing a little often, I actually completed more than I had planned and quicker.

Here are some simple tools to help get yourself motivated whatever the situation!

These ideas can be applied to any task, whether it be doing some DIY, finishing a presentation or having to do a long car journey.

1. Make a list of all the positive reasons for doing the task and list all the negatives if you didn't do the task.

2. Visualise the end result. Spend a few minutes with your eyes shut and imagine the task completed. What would you see, hear, smell and touch? How would you feel inside?

3. Write out a plan on how you could accomplish the task, in as much detail as possible.

If you are interested in exploring how your pain may be affecting your motivation and therefore your energy levels, why not contact me on 07770 672122 to arrange a free 45 min consultation to see how I may be able to help. There is no obligation to this session, however, by the end of it, I promise you will be excited to have clarity on the next steps you could take to reduce your pain and hence increase your energy levels.

Karl Hutchison

Empowering Women for life

Since 2010, Karl has empowered 1000's of women to feel great about themselves, improve their work life balance, regain control of their time, boost their confidence, boost their energy levels, understand their self-wealth, have an effective system of self-empowerment, spend precious time with those that they care about the most and live every day the way they want to for the rest of their lives. That is what Karl does for his clients; he empowers them for life.

Email: karl@nexusphysiques.com

Website: www.nexusphysiques.co.uk

Phone: +447972228433

How To Improve Your Energy

Empowering Women for life

Since 2010, Karl has empowered 1000's of women to feel great about themselves, improve their work life balance, regain control of their time, boost their confidence, boost their energy levels, understand their self-wealth, have an effective system of self-empowerment, spend precious time with those that they care about the most and live every day the way they want to for the rest of their lives. That is what Karl does for his clients; he empowers them for life.

Are you tired of having low energy levels day in and day out?

Here is a story about a client who has proven to be the perfect match to work with me (who then became a platinum full-time client).

One day a lady got in contact saying she was feeling distressed, overworked and exhausted day in and day out. She was at the end of her tether and was desperate to make a change in her life. For years she had had no time to herself, been given advice and read from multiple sources regarding nutrition in correlation with her goal. Not knowing what the right foods are to eat can be frustrating and sometimes too much knowledge can be dangerous. There were times when she was food shopping and she would not know what to buy.

After meeting with her new coach, she was taken through the Health Oracle; it exists to give the coach more insight to their client's lifestyle & mindset. It also helps determine what the best approach is for them. This was an eye opener for her; she discovered things about herself she had not known before. She came to realise her relationship with food was not the best. She struggled with undereating as she believed that there are more available bad then good foods and eating next to nothing is better than eating too much food.

The first thing they did was create small sustainable habits over a period before progressing. Habit 1 was to eat three meals per day; this had proven to be tricky at first, as the idea of eating three meals in a day brought up some red flags. The client was not sure if she would be able to get through this. Building up her food portions was challenging as she had a fear of gaining weight. To her excitement she started feeling like she was able to increase her food portions within 10 days; eating 3-4 meals per day, she had a new boost of confidence.

Now that the first habit was becoming second nature, the client was determined to tackle her sleeping challenge. She had a wearable fitness tracker, so she took the initiative and started tracking her sleeping patterns. On a regular basis, she would check her tracker and felt confident that even with her busy schedule, she could make the changes to improve here. By her regaining some control, it created a steady flow of positive changes into her daily routines. As this part of the journey progressed, they started to see a transformation take place in her. She was becoming the new person she had always wanted to be.

The next phase for her was to master her hunger and look at her schedule to find time for selfcare, anything from 15 - 20 minutes they believed would be a great start instead of trying to find too much time. Challenges did present themselves when learning more about food intake, but with their great teamwork, the client persevered and built a solid foundation. To summarise the first stage was about creating new daily habits and behaviours for the client to practise and build self-confidence thus making her dream more realistic.

As fate would have it her work life balance would start to shift and cause a slight pause in her progress. She struggled to find time to cook the foods she enjoyed, maintain physical activity and get enough sleep. She became distressed and was worried about having a downward spiral. But the foundations that were built proved to be highly effective, these were no longer new habits, but they had become second nature to her. This meant it was time for her coach to take the wheel for a little bit. This was done by taking additional time to micromanage her lifestyle, activity routine and offer more free nutrition choices. She experienced great relief by allowing someone else to take control of her fitness and nutrition so she could focus her attention where it was needed.

She found that it created up to an additional ten hours each week which worked out to be exactly what she wanted. This is where the working relationship excelled; she was no longer worried and becoming distressed by trying to do everything on her own any longer. Her coach was right there, by her side to support her with exactly what she needed every step of the way. By removing these additional stresses from her life her energy levels started to rebuild, nutrition was getting back on track and she started feeling positive again. This was a true display of leadership and teamwork between coach and client.

This is just one of many women I have helped transform their lives. She was empowered to have a foundation in place if life decided to throw her a curve ball.

If this story resonates with you and you want to live the rest of your life with an abundance of energy or you know someone who does, Karl is more then happy to make the time to have a conversation with you. Take note of his contact details, reach out and see if he can help you today.

Pauline Kirtley

Re-energise and be a transmitter

Pauline Kirtley is a retired primary class teacher, Headteacher of an Early Years Centre and Early Years Consultant. She is a facilitator of education, a mentor and coach. The well-being of children, families and colleagues have underpinned her educational career.

As a trained natural therapist, she now works with people who find themselves over-whelmed, have tension in their body and lack energy. Applying her system of energy channelling, Pauline enables people to feel calm and relaxed so they can release stress in their mind and body, be re-energised and have a better work-life balance.

Website: paulinekirtley.com

Phone: +44(0)7506692369

Email: paulinemkirtley@hotmail.com

LinkedIn: www.linkedin.com/in/paulinekirtley

Facebook: https://www.facebook.com/viryawellbeing

Teacher Or Juggler?

What if I told you that it is possible to be both an effective teacher *and* a talented juggler? Energise and be both! What if I told you that it is possible for teachers to manage the job they trained for, to regain their enthusiasm and to feel that they can have renewed energy enabling them to have a good work-life balance?

Many women in particular feel their life is a juggling act, balancing motherhood with employment. We are all jugglers at different points in our lives where our life seems to become a battle, a quagmire and we feel stressed.

I have been extremely fortunate to have had a rewarding 40 year career in education. I greatly valued the opportunity I had of making a difference to so many children's lives and that of their families. However, there was a point in my career when I began to feel that my energy was waning with the pressures and workload. In the many roles I held at that time: teacher, homemaker, mother and wife, this tiredness created a perception that I was indeed a poor juggler and not managing anything very well. I was experiencing a lack of energy, not due to the actual hours that I was working but because I was feeling overwhelmed.

Many teachers join the profession as they feel they have a particular calling, that they wish to teach for its rewards rather than for financial reasons and they regard it as a vocation. However, data suggests that within the teaching profession, there are a large number of teachers who are not continuing in a career in which they had invested time and money. This 'drop out' rate seems particularly high and Tapp explores this situation referring to the expression 'teacher burnout'. Tapp acknowledges that teachers are committed and work hard but emphasises the importance of teachers ensuring they have sufficient rest and time away from their work to help them to remain in their profession. The experience I had of not managing my energy levels effectively and feeling unable to manage the workload of teaching was not unique to me; it is clearly a systemic problem!

In my pursuit of a solution to my experience of a lack of energy, I became aware of the relationship between the mind and the body and how an imbalance in one can detrimentally affect the other. Stressful experiences, for example, can trigger a reaction in the body, ranging from a headache, to the more severe cases of developing an ulcer or high blood pressure. For me, waking up on the first day of a holiday with a cold was not unusual; this cycle was occurring to force my mind to 'stop and rest'!

Through research, experience and training, I found and developed a system to recharge my batteries at the end of each day. This system, using non-invasive energy healing, ensured that I gave myself time for self-care, preventing me from running on 'empty'. I found I was able to work more effectively, feel in control of my life, experience improved restful sleep and have a strengthened immune system. Humorously, this led to a college querying whether I ran on Duracell batteries!

Using this complementary therapy, I could often be found in the staff room helping colleagues who were suffering from back ache, tension or headaches. Channelling energy where it was needed and turning off stress hormones, enabled staff to feel relief. I recall one particular event, when a music teacher caught her leg on a metal bar that was protruding from a piano stool; a wooden handle had fallen off and was to be replaced. The injury was minor but caused a stinging sensation. I gave her leg attention using the healing I was using on myself, which helped to remove the pain and enabled her to feel calmer. The impact was so significant that she referred her elderly mother to me. Despite many medical appointments, there had been no solution to the pain her mother experienced when using stairs. After following a programme with me, in combination with any medication that had been prescribed, the lady found she was pain free and had greater mobility; she was able to manage using the staircase in her house again. Another significant situation involved a colleague in education whose daughter, although not a teacher, was experiencing a high level of stress in her work, as a consequence of low energy. She was on the verge of giving up her career. After I worked with her she was able to release tension and anxieties which were impacting on her energy levels. This enabled her to return to her profession, working and managing her time more effectively, and having renewed enthusiasm for a job she loved.

My programmes support conventional medicine and, using a holistic approach can provide the same benefits as a relaxing holiday – an ideal way to build your immune system and re-energise! Experiencing a deep level of rest enables bodies and minds to repair and rejuvenate themselves. Lives feel revitalised with this increased energy and life no longer feels a juggling act; enjoyment in a career can be rekindled.

The following extract from D H Lawrence's poem, 'We are Transmitters', epitomises to me how important it is to ensure energy is flowing through us, whatever we do.

We are Transmitters
As we live, we are transmitters of life.
And when we fail to transmit life, life fails to flow through us.

And if, as we work, we can transmit life into our work,
Life, still more life, rushes into us to compensate, to be ready
And we ripple with life through the days.
D H Lawrence

Do you feel your energy is blocked or is failing to flow and that life has become a struggle, lacking joy and fulfilment? Are you struggling with the demands of life and feeling that you are not managing your work-life balance? Regardless of your work, if you feel that you aren't recharging properly and you are slowly depleting yourself over time, please contact me and let us explore how I might be able to help you. There is a way to ensure you are a transmitter, whichever path you follow.

Claudia R Knights

London's most compassionate sleep specialist

Claudia is passionate about helping women sleep well. Claudia typically works with female solicitors, who are struggling to sleep, which leaves them too exhausted to perform well at work or to enjoy time with their family and friends. She helps them regain control of their bodies and reclaim their sleep so that they have the energy to thrive in their daily lives. Claudia's unique approach combines her expertise in craniosacral therapy with over a decade of experience teaching meditation classes and workshops. She helps clients get the sleep they need to feel empowered to flourish in their careers and delight in the moments they spend with their loved ones.

Claudia's introduction to complementary therapies began 17 years ago. At the time, she was pursuing a successful corporate career when she was struck with grave health issues that conventional medicine struggled to resolve. Her journey through an array of therapies led to craniosacral therapy, which made such a monumental difference to her quality of life that she was inspired to become a registered therapist herself.

Claudia also continues to work as a Development Director for the charity, Impetus, which helps young people from disadvantaged backgrounds get the support they need to succeed in school, work and life.

Claudia holds a Master of Engineering in Aeronautics and Astronautics. She is an enthusiastic student of Iyengar yoga and lives and works in London.

Email: claudia@claudiarknights.com

Why Am I Exhausted?

What if I told you that you already hold the key to a treasure trove of boundless energy? Yet every morning you find yourself asking, 'Why am I exhausted? I've only just woken up!' Do you wake up with little or no energy, feeling that you haven't slept at all, even when you've had eight hours of sleep? Or perhaps you get by on five hours and just accept feeling tired as you push through the day. For many of us, we continue in this way until we have no energy at all, and our bodies and minds come to a dramatic stop. Sound familiar? This certainly describes my experience.

I spent years in a fast-moving corporate career doing exciting work, and consistently working 14-plus hour days even on the weekends, flying every week. I had struggled with sleep for some time and it had been worsening. Soon, a good night was four hours of sleep. I was exhausted and other areas of my life deteriorated too. I had a poor diet; I was overweight; I didn't exercise; I had no time for family and friends. It was just a question of time before I had forced my body to say - enough! In the years that followed, I suffered from anxiety, depression, a crippling fear of leaving my home, gut issues that just wouldn't resolve and zero energy. I'd hit rock bottom, trapped in a prison of despair, and eventually needed psychiatric intervention. So for the first time, I sought help from complementary health practitioners as I didn't want to remain stuck in poor health and on powerful medications with a barrage of unwelcome side-effects. The road back was long and at times, torturous. I struggled through a divorce, severe symptoms caused by the transition to menopause (the proposed solution to which was hormone replacement therapy (HRT) at 37 - surely there was an alternative), and more health problems. A change was necessary!

I have since changed my entire lifestyle, encompassing career, diet, exercise, spirituality and most importantly sleep. I came across craniosacral therapy, a gentle and powerful approach that first helped me manage my health challenges and has since resolved some of these completely. It also helped me get better sleep, which was fundamental to putting my life back together. I was so blown away by the results this therapy created for me that I completed the training and embarked on a career change. I now use this approach in my work to help others who are struggling with sleep. Today, I'm passionate about supporting people to sleep well so that they can restore their bodies and minds, and create the vitality that helps them feel empowered to flourish in their daily lives.

As you can imagine, my journey has given me deep insights into my clients' experiences of lacking energy. I know first-hand that a big challenge we face, even though we recognise we're not getting enough sleep, is thinking we're doing okay because we're busy functioning. This is a misconception which is partly due to an effect seen in sleep research, known as baseline resetting. As our bodies become accustomed to getting less sleep and functioning at a suboptimal level, our brain recalibrates this tired state as our new standard. We fail to recognise that we are sleep-deprived and the impact this is having on our performance, declining health, career and relationships. The result - we can be exhausted and not performing at all well, but have not identified the problem, so we don't seek a solution. So it's vital to recognise that if you're not sleeping well, to change that. The first step is to find specialist support, as getting better sleep can provide the boost you need to reclaim your life. In the words of one client *"I slept so well last night, am full of beans and alert this morning. Totally different to me last weekend when I just couldn't get on with anything. Thank you!!!!"*

Because we don't see the signs that we're not getting enough sleep, I often ask clients to describe their experience of jet lag. They recall being tired but unable to sleep at night, lacking energy and feeling drowsy during the day, having difficulty concentrating, exhaustion, headaches, feeling irritable, short-tempered, lethargic and lacking motivation. When I ask them to compare this list with the reasons they've come to my clinic, it's quite a revelation for them to see how closely this mirrors their current situation.

This powerful insight makes it easier to take another valuable step in getting your sleep back on track. You see, modern life for most of us means that we sleep and wake at very different times each day and then sleep-in to catch up at the weekends. (By the way, while we can benefit to some extent with a lie-in, this just doesn't work as a long-term solution because sleep is essential to the regeneration of the healthy functioning of our brains.) Our bodies have a natural internal clock that regulates our sleep-wake cycle known as the circadian rhythm, which repeats roughly every 24 hours. Crossing time zones or going to bed and waking up at different times each day can disrupt this internal time-keeper. We then experience the 'jet lag' described above. So, how do we combat this daily 'jet lag'? Set our clock! That means going to bed and waking up at the same time every day, including the weekends.

Clients often ask, If I'm tired in the day and struggling with these 'jet lag' effects, why not take a power nap, to see me through? Naps can be an effective energy booster but will not make up for the impact of poor sleep. If we need one to get through the day, then something is out of balance. For one of my clients, Michelle, a scheduled nap, fixed in the diary every working day was the way she survived the week, a sure sign that something was wrong.

Michelle, a successful business owner in her early 60s, had been struggling with sleep for several years. She'd lost her enjoyment of life, was always tired and forgetful. The business was becoming an uphill struggle. Michelle assumed her lack of energy was age-related and felt that a nap was embedded in her working life now. After our sessions together, to get her back to quality sleep, Michelle felt super energised. She embarked on new projects; redecorated; took a long-postponed road trip with her husband; her relationship with her adult children felt stronger, and interestingly her business was thriving. Those challenging clients that she was on the verge of firing were now manageable. And the naps? She didn't need them!

So is there any value in taking naps to boost our energy levels? Yes, if used effectively, naps can be an incredible boost to our mood and cognitive ability, increasing creativity, working memory and problem-solving, but this will only work well if you're already getting enough sleep. The golden rule of taking a nap is that it must be short. Sleep research led by NASA formulated the concept of the power nap and its benefits, and more recent research has shown that the optimal time for a nap is 10 to 20 minutes. Remember, although there are benefits to napping, the main factor affecting our alertness, vigilance and vitality is the amount of sleep in 24 hours. And for those of us who can't seem to sleep in the day, taking the same time to close your eyes and switch off from the outside world produces the same benefits.

Sleep is fundamental to having the energy levels we need to enjoy life. For me, it has been key to reclaiming my zest for life and beating depression, and I've seen the far-reaching benefits for clients like Michelle again and again. First, take that all-important step of deciding to get support.

If you would like to know how to change the status quo and build the energy levels you know you need to bring your best version of yourself to the world, email me at claudia@claudiarknights.com for a complimentary 30-minute call.

Christine Laidlaw

Pilates & Movement Specialist

Christine Laidlaw is a mumpreneur, Pilates and Movement Specialist and Director of The Chatsworth Studio a Pilates and wellbeing studio in Cheam Village in Surrey, England.

Christine has had a successful career in financial I.T. support. During this time Christine had a car accident, which damaged her back and caused a long-term whiplash injury. Pilates helped her to recover, repair her back and become pain free. A passionate convert to the benefits of Pilates she quit her job in I.T. to train as a Pilates teacher. This enabled her to pursue her ambitions of building her own business at the same time as creating a better work/life balance and to raise a family.

The Chatsworth Studio has grown from its initial beginnings in her dining room at home into church halls and finally to a modern, well equipped pilates and wellbeing Studio. In her 20 years of practice she has helped hundreds of her clients resolve their back pain, increase their energy and improve their confidence.

Website: www.chatsworthstudio.com

Email: christine@christinelaidlaw.com

Phone: +44(0)7814 003679

Facebook: @chatsworthstudio

Twitter: @chatsworthstudi

Instagram: chatsworth.studio

Do You Feel Like You Are 'Walking Through Treacle'?

If you answered 'yes' to the above question you are not alone. Some days we feel great and we can conquer the world but others we might just want to crawl under the duvet to sleep. We all have unbalanced hormones at some point in our lives. It could be menopause or burn out. Tiredness and "walking through treacle" is incredibly frustrating and unpredictable.

Do you feel like this sometimes? Are you trying to look after your child whilst feeling like this? Or just going to work?

It is a big challenge. It may be that you are in that burn out phase due to pressures at work, burning the candle at both ends or illness. Taking time out to rest and relax is essential to recovery. Pacing yourself and making minor tweaks to your daily routine can help.

Finding a little time for yourself to switch off and do Pilates can help you gain energy through the movement and mind body connection. I have found a little exercise and lots of rest helps immensely. So it may be that you can attend a Pilates class and only do 3 reps of each exercise instead of 10 or you may have private lessons and be able to shorten the lesson and have it adapted especially for you to work with your condition or energy levels and how you feel on that day. Maybe start with a meditation class to relax and revitalise? The breath breathes oxygen and life into your muscles giving you renewed energy and vigour. It helps the body to repair itself and operate more effectively using less energy as you will be using the correct movement patterns to facilitate better movement. I have found that looking after children is the most challenging task. If they are able to make their own snacks or sandwiches this is a great help along with the TV or computer! You can't always play with them every minute of the day especially when you are ill or incredibly tired. Divide the day into chunks of time when you book a meeting with yourself to have a rest or sleep.

A good balanced diet and vitamin supplementation can help with the symptoms as can practising Pilates and the mind body connection, breathing on a regular basis. There are various diets that are suggested for a specific illnesses or conditions so it is always worth investigating and consulting a qualified nutritionist or doctor to check out your options and whether the diet is right for you. Pilates has helped me to keep my muscles strong and supple despite being incredibly difficult to perform at times when you are exceptionally tired and 'walking through treacle'. It may be that you can only manage 5 minutes of Pilates a day and a few breathing exercises, or you may be able to do a whole class and then your body decides it wants to sleep for a week! Pacing yourself is key in this instance as you need to keep a balance of essential activity e.g. looking after children, going to work if possible along with looking after yourself and getting enough rest.

I have helped numerous people regain their energy and get back on track through Pilates. Read my story below about how I managed to increase my energy levels.

Christine's Story

I have chronic fatigue and M.E. (Myalgic Encephalitis) both of which are little understood conditions. Also, I suffer with Endometriosis, a painful condition that causes cells similar to those which grow in the uterus to grow in other areas of the body. Little is known with the causes of these conditions and they can affect all areas of your life. It makes you very tired and every task is like climbing a mountain when you are ill. My M.E. possibly managed to get to the level it did due to having a baby, looking after him full time, running a Pilates Studio full time and not taking any time for me. During this time I unknowingly caught a virus from my sons nursery which adults don't usually catch, I had two operations to fix the Endometriosis and birth issues all the while with my hormones fluctuating. I should have slowed down! I continued to teach Pilates, eat a good diet and take vitamin supplements to keep my energy levels up and to calm the inflammation down. My M.E. possibly started due to the viruses and inflammation that I had. It has now calmed down considerably. M.E. and chronic fatigue could possibly be caused by a number of things and you may have an additional issue alongside the M.E. I was lucky as some M.E. people are bed bound for months with very little medical help. Already having information on nutrition and supplementation helped me a lot. I am continuing to improve my Pilates practice and teaching as there is always more to learn and I work with my energy levels in a more paced way now.

No matter whether you just need a bit of a boost or are recovering from an injury or illness Pilates can help you to feel more energised and uplifted. The exercises are tailored to your energy levels, ability and goals, whether that means you do a very short exercise session and add meditation and breathing to improve your muscular strength if you have something like chronic fatigue, or you want to gain peak physical fitness and go for it to improve your energy and endurance.

A great exercise to do to increase your focus and energy is to sit down and take nice big deep breaths into your tummy to increase your oxygen flow to your muscles and focus the mind on your breathing. This helps you to take 5 minutes out and relax and switch off. You will then be ready for anything!

I typically work with ladies from 35 to 45 years of age with back pain, who are passionate about having an active life, gain confidence, increase energy, want to reduce their pain and return to their favourite sport.

Would you like to increase your energy levels by trying a Pilates class? The Pilates class can be at The Chatsworth Studio in Cheam Village or in your own home via Zoom or Skype. If you are in pain a private 121 is advised as you would get more specialist attention and I can work out a specific programme for you to get the best out of your sessions, progress and have more energy.

To find out if we are a match and how I can help you why not try a FREE Private 121 class?

Jane McDowell

Bristol's Favourite Drug-free Migraine & Headache Solution

2019 winner of the Heart Centred Business Award for Outstanding Service, Jane has 20 years' experience of helping people get out of pain. Her work focuses on drug-free pain solutions primarily working with people suffering from debilitating migraines.

Jane's transformational work with migraine sufferers means that they see a significant reduction in the number of migraines they have and the intensity of the pain they experience. As a result, they regain their confidence, energy and focus so they flourish and succeed in their relationships and careers.

Website: www.drugfreemigrainesolutions.com

Email: jane@drugfreemigrainesolutions.com

Phone: +447779023117

Pain Killers Or Energy Robbers?

Imagine this, you're at work one day and then you notice a horrible sicky feeling in the back of your head and neck, and what's more, you realise you can't see properly. A moment of panic flashes through your mind, 'Have I got my migraine medication with me or at least some paracetamol or ibuprofen?' You try to stay calm, make your apologies and leave work hoping that you make it home before it kicks off big time.

You muster all your energy to get home and when you get there you crumple into a heap because of the intense pain in your head. You take more pain killers. You've hardly got the energy to find your meds and get some water. You seek out your bedroom, draw the blinds and crawl under the duvet knowing that you should really eat something with your meds but the thought of going back to the kitchen is like being asked to climb Everest.

If you're lucky, someone else is at home and they come to see if you're ok and ask if you need anything. You've got no energy so you can barely respond.

Someone brings you something to eat and the best you can do is grunt in appreciation. You don't have the energy to sit up and eat what they've brought you because you know that the slightest movement will intensify the excruciating pain in your head.

Then the nausea strikes and you pray that you don't vomit because when you do your head feels like it will literally burst open.

Lights, sunshine, daylight, computer screens, phones, bathroom lights, soft lamps, all of them stab at your eyes and turn up the volume of the pain and nausea you're feeling. They must all be banished from your world.

In the meantime, those painkillers you've taken, urgh you're starting to feel fuzzier in the head and more nauseous. You're feeling utterly exhausted, you're so tired, trying to get comfortable so that you don't have to move because every slight movement increases the pain. Oh the pain, surely it's not possible to stay alive with this level of pain? You try to sleep in the hope that you can switch off from the pain and the nausea.

You sleep in fits and starts; your whole body aches. You desperately want this all to stop. The storm rages in your head and throughout your body for another 2 days until finally you begin to feel human again and the pain subsides and you can once again gaze at the outside world or turn on the bathroom light without fear of the light. The pain ebbs away and you spend 2 more days feeling utterly wiped out and exhausted.

At last you feel normal again and you resume your daily life, but now you've been joined by a constant fear that the storm that was your migraine might return. There's a little voice in your head constantly asking if there are any signs of an oncoming headache, vigilantly on the lookout for any changes in your vision or discomfort from lights.

And so it is that at the merest suggestion of a headache you start taking painkillers, even if you don't have any pain yet. But guess what? This preventative action doesn't stop you getting another migraine and a week later you're going through the whole excruciating scenario all over again. And so your life is reduced to a cycle of being in pain or living in fear of being in pain again.

A few months later you notice that you feel tired and exhausted pretty much all the time and this is impacting on your enjoyment of life. Going to work is a drag, you start missing exercise classes, socialising with friends and spending good quality time with your partner. I know this because this was what my life was like in my 30s and it's what life is like for many of my clients when they first come to see me.

This constant exhaustion and lack of energy is caused not just by the migraines but by the painkillers that we take. In the long term the painkillers rob us of our energy more than the migraines do. How so? I hear you ask. Yes some painkillers, codeine for example, say on the packet that they can cause drowsiness. What they don't tell you on the packet in plain English is that when taken regularly pain killers are harmful to our gut health (whether that be over the counter drugs like paracetamol and ibuprofen or prescription pain killers like codeine and sumatriptan).

Why, you might ask, is gut health so important and what has that got to do with our energy levels? Well, essentially there are many toxins in the drugs that we take and these have a detrimental effect on the good bacteria in our gut. When the good bacteria become unhealthy and depleted this disrupts the function of our gut and allows the toxins that our body is trying to get rid of to pass back through the lining of our gut and into our system. In simple terms this sends our immune system into overdrive and produces more inflammation in our bodies. Inflammation is a cause of pain and here lies the irony in taking pain killers because in the long-term they will cause us more pain and negatively affect our energy levels.

Poor gut health also affects our mood because Serotonin, which is one of our main feel good hormones, is generated in the gut and when our gut health is compromised, we don't produce enough serotonin so we end up with low mood as well as low energy.

When I realised the importance of gut health and the impact that taking so many pain killers was having on my general health and my energy levels I set out on a journey to learn how to manage my migraines without drugs. In so doing I developed my own unique drug free solution for reducing the number of migraines I had and for managing the pain. I'm now on a mission to help as many people as I can to do the same and I've helped hundreds of people to regain their energy and get back control of their lives.

Improving gut health is just one of the areas that I work on with my clients so that they regain their energy, have fewer migraines and manage their pain drug free. If you are taking pain killers regularly then I'd recommend having a chat with your doctor to review your medication and also to look for alternative ways to manage your pain so that you avoid falling into a cycle of pain and low energy. Good gut health is key to a healthy body, good mood and feeling energetic. If you'd like some support and suggestions on what you could do, feel free to drop me an email or give me a call as I'd be very happy to explore how to get you out of pain and feeling more energised.

Hazel Macfarlane

Hazel Macfarlane worked for over 20 years as an Architect before shifting her attentions from buildings to bodies. Challenged to resolve over 15 years of low energy levels meant she applied her perspective of the 'bigger picture' to discover her fascination of the body's intelligence and how to communicate with it.

Using techniques based on 1000's of years of learning, she works with the body's subtle energy systems to help people connect with what their body wants to say. As a Health Architect she helps clients unravel puzzling, long-term health issues to bring back energy flow and balance.

Company: Designed to be

Email: hazel@designedtobe.co.uk

Website: www.designedtobe.co.uk

Have You Ever Wished Your Body Could Speak?

Have you ever been so frustrated with your energy levels that you have been going round in circles looking at different techniques, diet, sleep patterns, time commitments and still haven't found an answer? Do you get that sinking feeling when your children ask you to take them to the park, your partner wants to go on an evening out or your job needs you to be more active? Is this the kind of chatter going on in your head every day:

> "Will I have enough energy to make it until lunch break?"
>
> "Can I say yes, and cancel if I don't feel up to it?"
>
> "I will be fine! If I manage an hour on the sofa after lunch I'll be able to collect the kids."

Well, if so, then I'm also sure you have asked the question,

"Why can't my body talk and tell me what it needs?"

My name is Hazel Macfarlane from *Designed to be* and I discovered that your body CAN speak, you CAN find a solution and there IS a way of hearing what your body says AND what it needs. Using techniques based on 1000's of years of knowledge it is possible to bring your energy back into balance.

Let me share with you how I discovered this amazing possibility. I trained and worked for 20 years as an architect, had a stressful workload in the commercial sector in London and latterly ran an office in Berlin. I had just started married life when I suddenly had a series of panic attacks and anxiety spikes that stopped me in my tracks. From one day to the next I couldn't manage to go out, drive the car or even cope with daily jobs. It was incredibly frightening, not to mention puzzling, and I looked into every possible option to get back my energy and my life. However, this led to a long process that spanned almost 15 years. Yes, 15 years of ups and downs in energy levels.

I began to feel like I would never get to the bottom of it and had resigned myself to just coping! I tried everything including many alternative therapies and some worked for a time but then I would have a relapse. However, I then discovered one that changed everything. After all this time of mental analysis, worry and questioning of my situation (Was I going mad, was I a hypochondriac?), I discovered a technique that removed my brain from the equation and went straight to my body.........I was hooked. This technique talks directly to the body's energy systems and so allows the body an opportunity to explain where it is struggling and where it needs help.

So why is this technique exciting? Well, if you have suffered for many years with energy issues then you will have tried many different therapies and had many confusing diagnosis. Why try this one? Well, perhaps think of it like this:

If you have a problem with a service or product who

would you rather speak to, the customer call-centre or the head of the company? With health, there are many amazing practitioners who have experience of specific issues and if you find the right one to match your problem then great, but as each of us is unique with different life experiences. Put that into the mix and the chances of finding the right help can take a long time. Just like the call to the call-centre. However, if you had the option of going directly to the head of the company, wouldn't you take it?

Our body IS the head of the company and you can talk directly to it. There is no equipment involved but just using simple arm and leg movements it is possible to get an energetic response that communicates with the body. Then using specific exercises, you can support your systems and bring your energy back into balance.

Now I make this sound simple, but as you know when one part of your health starts to suffer it affects other areas and there is always a knock on effect as the body naturally attempts to survive and find balance. You are a complex organism with many systems working together and if the issues have been going on for some time there may be a number of layers and static that have built up just allowing you to get through the day. It means the body is giving out confusing signals. By using energy-testing techniques to talk to the body it is possible to remove the static and empower you to understand the body's voice. When this happens, not only does your energy start flowing but having a greater awareness of your personal blocks means you don't repeat old patterns and you learn to trust your body again.

You see, the first stage is having the tool to communicate with the body but the next part is to understand the vocabulary it is using. The techniques and mindset I apply have all have one thing in common, they look at the body as a whole, the bigger picture. As an Architect, you are trained to work with the overall design. To learn about each of the component parts and understand how they function, fit together and identify where there are problems. Unlike buildings, our bodies have an inner intelligence and it is communicating with this intelligence that makes it so exciting. Energy Medicine is rooted in traditional teachings that identify ALL the body's subtle energy systems, how they communicate and how they work together to keep us surviving and thriving.

To illustrate this better let me tell you a client's story. A lady came to me 2 months after returning home from travelling. She needed to be hospitalised for suspected Pneumonia and followed by many rounds of antibiotics, she was still struggling with low energy and poor breathing. She was developing side effects to the medications too. The combination had left her unable to work, study or even go out with friends. After the 2nd visit, where her body was responding to the dialogue and exercises, she reported stopping the car on the way home to cry. She felt she could suddenly breathe more deeply than she had in months. It wasn't a sudden healing but the start of a process that helped her understand how her body was struggling and where she could best support it. This also included supporting her system with simple exercises when she needed to take medication, minimising the side effects. All this finally gave her the energy to get out, see friends and start working again.

I am passionate about helping people unravel the root cause of puzzling, unresolved health conditions.

Our bodies are designed to heal themselves given the right circumstances. When we have a disease it is our body's way of highlighting a problem.

"Energy is the language the body speaks" - *Donna Eden*.

By learning the language it speaks, it means that it doesn't have to scream before we take notice.

TALK TO THE BODY, LEARN THE LANGUAGE and REGAIN THAT INNER TRUST AND KNOWING YOU WERE BORN WITH.

My clients are generally women in their 40s and 50s who have been struggling for years with unresolved low energy levels. Committing to a regular schedule and appointments is overwhelming, affecting family life and work. It is the first thought they wake up to and the last thought before going to bed. Working to understand the body's dialogue helps clients shift old patterns. This brings back the energy so they can finally make those commitments to children, partners and/or work with ease and freedom.

Do you, or someone you know, wish to let go of the fear controlling your life and instead look forward to a relaxed outlook on life? We are designed to be healthy living organisms. If you wish to discover what your body is telling you, then please get in touch.

Lisa Moore

No 1 Back Pain practitioner in Warwickshire

Lisa has been successfully treating back pain since 2001 with clients from all over the UK. Having delivered more than 100 lectures to companies and associations, Lisa has won the Leamington Business Award for Customer Excellence and was Runner Up in the best small business category. She held the contract for providing sports massage to the WWE wrestlers when touring the UK and provides massage at corporate and sporting events nationwide.

Lisa gets people moving again pain free. Are you interested in transforming your body so you can live your life again? If so, contact Lisa.

Website: www.leamingtontherapycentre.co.uk

Email: lisa@leamingtontherapycentre.co.uk

Phone: +44(0)1926 833003

Do You Always Feel Like You Have No Energy?

Have you ever thought how your posture makes you feel?

It's a good idea to get into the habit of checking your posture as this has a major impact on your energy levels.

I'm treating more and more people with lack of energy but who are also experiencing back pain. The main reason for this is poor posture. This can be helped and prevented with knowledge, education and realignment of the body through treatment, strength training and rehabilitation.

Many years ago I was in the corporate world and spent a lot of time at an office desk working on a PC. The pain that I endured in my my back was unbelievable. Tight upper back muscles as hard as a board, constant headaches and lower back pain from slouching. I was constantly exhausted; my breathing became restricted due to my poor posture, my energy levels were low as I wasn't getting enough oxygen into my lungs, I was always tired and constantly yawning and I felt 'burnt out'. I would admire people I met always full of energy and noticed they all had something in common; an upright and relaxed posture. I would ask myself, '...How do you get a posture like that?'

I'd developed an interest in health, wellness and the human body (which led me to my career change a few years later) and was reading an article about habits, behaviour and muscle memory. Did you know it takes an average of 66 days for a new behaviour to become automatic? Great I thought to myself, I'm going to start with my first wish, to be able to sit down without crossing my legs. I put a post-it note on my computer screen which read 'uncross legs'. Whenever I crossed my legs I'd see this and uncross them. It wasn't too long before this became automatic. Soon after I was implementing others in the same manner to help me improve my posture and before long I noticed a dramatic improvement. My energy levels had started to increase, I was breathing better and I was a calmer person. Still the unhappiness in my career was slowly eating away at me physically, mentally and emotionally and I was taking this out on those around me. Finally, I decided to take the plunge and do a course that would lead me to my desired career. Now I have my own thriving business in Leamington Spa and work from my clinic with my associates. We help others to energise and revitalise themselves and teach them how they can adjust their lives to make this possible.

This generation has a seen a big shift in work practice with an increased use of technology and hours spent travelling long distances in cars. Striving to meet deadlines and targets affects us mentally and physically. The modern woman juggling work and family life puts herself under pressure to do it all perfectly. In turn these lifestyle changes have altered us leaving little or no time to focus on and nurture ourselves.

This change in lifestyle has consequences; these include:

Poor posture, leading to physical stress in the body which in turn leads to mental stress

- Poor hunched posture reducing lung capacity, leading to shallow breathing or panic attacks
- Reduced lung capacity leading to a depletion of oxygen in the body causing fatigue
- Fatigue, causing impaired decision making and judgement, poor concentration and mood swings
- Lack of mental stimulation, leading to boredom or even poor memory
- Lack of physical stimulation, causing low energy levels leading to muscle weakness, or even obesity
- Poor posture causing compression of the stomach and bowels, leading to poor digestion
- Poor digestion leading to a reduced immune system leading to poor health
- Bad diet with a lack of nutrients leading to poor health or even obesity.

When your bones and joints are in correct alignment, it allows the muscles to be used as they are intended. In other words, the muscles don't have to work so hard to do what they're supposed to do, leaving you with more energy to do the other things in your life you want to do.

"You'll feel happier and more energetic with a good posture" is something I'm always telling my clients. Client A came to see me after experiencing panic attacks. She was in chronic pain in her upper back which she had endured for months, having migraines on a daily basis, feeling constantly tired with no energy.

She was in a high-powered job sitting at a desk all day and was finding it difficult to concentrate. Her productivity had reduced and she was afraid of not reaching her targets. More to the point she was afraid of not providing for her family. Her poor posture was causing physical stress on her body; all she could focus on was the pain which was causing her mental stress. This was brought on by her heavy workload. She was sitting for long periods of time trying to get all of her work completed which meant she suffered more physical stress.

Her back was so painful to touch that the first session was just to introduce her muscles to the changes they were about to go through. With an exercise plan in place, advice on diet, sleep and how to set up her workstation she noticed a big difference after just one treatment.

With still a long way to go we went on a journey together to increasing her energy levels, eliminating the muscular pain, realigning and strengthening her posture and educating her on the things she could do to help herself. Within a short period of time we had eradicated all of her symptoms and she was back enjoying her work and family life again with more energy and free from pain.

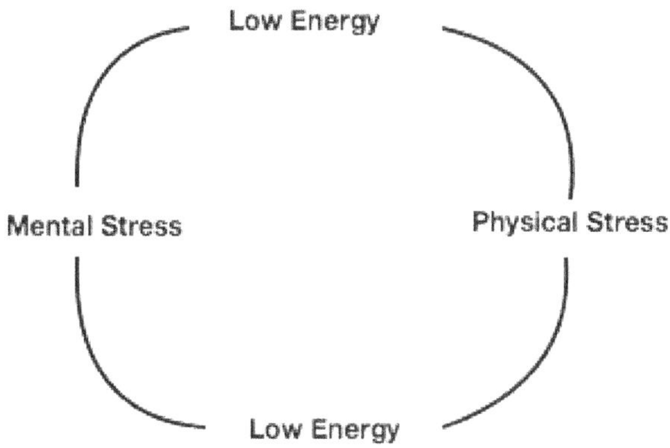

5 Top tips to energise yourself.

- Remember to ask yourself throughout the day 'How am I sitting/standing?' Run through the checklist of ears, shoulders, hips and feet
- Get moving, keep fit with cardio & strength and rebalance with yoga or pilates
- Eat the right food
- Stay hydrated with water
- Have regular maintenance massage

Testimonials

After years of back pain, and seeing lots of different specialists from chiropractors, acupuncturists and physiotherapists who haven't been able to relieve me of my aches and pains, Lisa has been working her magic on me for the last 4 weeks and my pain has greatly reduced from the first session. I feel very confident in Lisa's skills and I'm very grateful we crossed paths. If you suffer with back pain, I highly recommend a visit to Lisa.

Liz Wood

After two appointments with Lisa my condition greatly improved and my movement is now 100% better, I would strongly recommend anyone with back pain see Lisa as she is extremely thorough and effective with her results.

John Wills

Irma Prins

Helping kids move freely

Irma has been unlocking people's energy by helping them to move the way they are designed to for 3 decades now. When she started applying her physiotherapy skills to young children, whilst they were positioned on a walking horse (hippotherapy/ equine facilitated physiotherapy), she was amazed about how much progress they made in their development and how quickly they achieved it. Since then she has been keen to see as many children benefit from this as possible.

Therefore, she has helped shape the future of hippotherapy/ equine facilitated therapy and the education of therapists through her roles in the committee of the Chartered Physiotherapists in Therapeutic Riding and Hippotherapy (CPTRH), UK. She has served on this Specialist Interest Group for 8 years. She also took part in the first European Equine Facilitated Therapy Network meeting in Prague in 2019, where decisions were made about the definition of Equine Facilitated Therapy, and a plan was developed on how to bring all the expertise in Europe together under one umbrella. Irma runs lectures for other professionals.

Irma is based in the Midlands, UK and expanding! Out of area? Don't worry. Sessions without horses can be done on-line.

Email: irma@irmaprins.com
Facebook: FreedomPhysioServices
Phone: +44 7402 825904

What If I Told You That Positioning Children Well Gives Them Energy?

Is your child struggling to move? Would you love it if your child had the energy to do what he or she really wants to do, instead of using it all to stay upright and fight unwanted movement? Let me show you what can be done through my 3 step system.

I typically see children between 1-3 years old who have difficulties developing their movement skills such as lifting their head when lying on their tummy, sitting independently to play with their toys, standing or walking. I help them to gain more control over their postures, so they can use their bodies to move more efficiently without wasting energy, gain independence and engage with the world around them with a smile on their faces.

For almost 30 years I've worked with people with brain injuries, and the one thing that stands out to me is that people save energy when they move in the way they are designed to move! This starts with good posture, and it applies to everyone, regardless of age and abilities. Below you will find the 3 step system I have developed through my training and experiences.

Step 1 is to find out what is stopping your child from achieving the right posture for the movement he or she wants to do, and to solve this. This could be a lack of flexibility or strength. Step 2 is to practice the posture while moving. Step 3 is to make it even harder by adding more challenges so the new skill becomes automatic. I applied this system to my own movement problems when I wanted to improve my horse riding skills. I surprised myself with how much fitter I felt when I managed to balance gracefully on the horse instead of bouncing up and down like a bag of potatoes.

You can support your child by always making sure that he/she is well positioned in their everyday activities. This might mean a verbal correction or a gentle touch to help them achieve this. It could be placing toys just in the right place or it could be that they need support in the form of special equipment.

I would love to tell you some stories about how I use this 3 step system with young children on horseback, because that works better and even more quickly!!! There are some elements that being on a horse adds to the equation, such as fun (if you like horses), stimulation of all the senses, and a set of unique repetitive movements, which all contribute to the learning of a new skill. *Of course, using horses in therapy is a skill which needs to be learned by trained professionals. It also requires a dedicated trained team of assistants to keep the child safe, and special horses which are selected for their temperament and for their movements.*

The first story is of 2 year old Lily.

Lily was born 5 weeks early and she spent a lot of time in hospital due to health issues. She wasn't able to develop normally during this time, which meant that she learned all her movements in a slightly different way. Her back muscles were much stronger than her tummy muscles, so she tended to use these instead of her tummy and legs (step 1- identifying the cause, in this case weak tummy and leg muscles). This abnormal way of moving meant that she was struggling to stand by herself and let go of support to take steps on her own. This is when I was called in.

Firstly, I set up a programme with her parents and the nursery staff to help her gain more control over her tummy muscles (resolving the identified cause of non-alignment to complete step 1). She then practised that control in all the positions she used for playing (step 2). We also taught her how to use her legs for standing up etcetera. Everyone worked brilliantly with her so results came straight away.

We then went to the riding centre and, after introducing Lily to the pony, we placed her on top in the right position facing the tail end (step 1). We then asked the horse to walk (step 2). This movement would gently push her off balance encouraging her to use her tummy muscles to steady herself. Due to the many repetitions of the movements, her muscles became stronger and stronger. When she could keep her balance facing backwards, we moved her into a forward facing position on the horse. This was more challenging for Lily (step 3).

When Lily started working on the horse, her improvement at home accelerated. Within a few weeks her mum reported that she was walking loads around by herself. Of course this was less tiring for her than pulling on furniture to move about, and it gave her independence too.

Not all changes are so dramatic and quick, but the

following story demonstrates that even changes that seem small can make a huge difference.

Kieran was a 6 year old boy who had weakness and lack of control in most of his body, including all his limbs and head. It was very hard for him to sit upright in his wheelchair, so he had cushioned supports on the side to help him with this. He was unable to keep his head still long enough for him to fix his eyes on an object or make eye contact with a person without completely turning it. His head needed to be supported for feeding and it took a long time to eat a meal. He was unable to speak and used facial expressions to communicate.

During our sessions we placed Kieran nicely onto his tummy facing the tail of the horse (step 1). The movement of the walking horse made him strengthen the muscles of his upper body and neck (step 2), and occasionally he was able to lift his head for short periods and give us a big smile (step 3). Unfortunately Kieran was not able to attend sessions as regularly as I would have liked him to in order to gain their full benefit, but they did help him to sit much better in his wheelchair. The time it took for him to have a meal was reduced by half! After two years he was able to steady his head enough for him to move his eyes and use an eye-controlled communication device. He didn't have to rely on his mum anymore to make his wishes known!

These stories are wonderful illustrations of how the 3 step system can help kids to develop a strong and secure posture allowing them to save energy so they can walk, play, eat or communicate independently.

If you think that someone you know might benefit from saving energy, using this method, then please, email me on irma@irmaprins.com or phone +44 7402

825904 so we can schedule a free 1 hour consultation (To ADD: *to find out what areas to work on to achieve the best possible outcome).* Non-horsey sessions are also possible on-line.

And, like Kieran's mum says, 'the younger kids can start, the better the outcome'.

Simon Rogers

The Feel Better Coach

Simon has worked with thousands of clients across Europe for over 15 years. He has helped them solve long-standing stress-related upper back and neck pain leading them to live more successful and fulfilling lives.

He's found that working with people as people, physically, emotional and mentally rather than focusing only on their symptoms allows them to work at the root cause. This provides them with not only a lasting solution to their pain but means that they can fall in love with a life that they are now consciously creating.

What would you be able to do if you were able to solve your pain for good?

Website: www.restoreyourbodynow.co.uk

Email: simon@restoreyourbodynow.co.uk

Phone: +44(0)20 8396 6668

The Part You Are Missing To Feeling Energetic!

What if I told you that having energy has little to do with the number of hours sleep you get or the number or type of calories that you eat? Intrigued? Let me explain...

Do you remember when you first fell in love or finally got the client or the job you had always wanted? You were so present and in love with life that you didn't need anywhere near as much sleep or food and yet you still felt far more energetic than you usually do! So how did this happen? What are we missing? In a word, your mindset.

There are two 'types' of mindset: a 'growth' and a 'fixed' mindset. Simply put, a growth mindset comes from a place of development. Here the belief is that we and/or others can develop any ability. A fixed mindset comes from a place of judgement where we believe that we and/or other's abilities are fixed and set in stone.

We often have a mix of growth and fixed mindsets in different areas of our lives and most are subconscious. In my experience, a fixed mindset is self-created, often as a way for us try and understand the world around us and how we can function in it. Ultimately, it is a story that isn't absolutely true and a limited perspective that can cause friction because it doesn't match up to the reality of life. For example, did you once believe that you had to win everything in order to feel self-worth? I know I did. I struggled to listen to feedback and always took it as personal criticism. Due to a strong will to win, I was a high achiever, but I didn't have any self-worth. My self-worth was hollow like a balloon; with one piercing bit of feedback it would deflate. My self-worth felt like a wrinkled shell of a balloon on the floor. Does that resonate with you?

The emotion that drives this pattern of judgement within a fixed mindset is fear. Fear of failure, fear of success, fear of rejection and most importantly, fear of not being enough. Fear can energise you but it's a wild stallion that if you aren't careful will send you flying off the back of it and crashing to the earth.

In my experience, it is difficult to not feel fear. One way to avoid facing your fears is to numb. But just because you have got your hands over your eyes, it doesn't mean that fear is not standing there right in front of you! Also, you cannot selectively numb. So, you must also numb every other emotion with the fear including happiness. So, there's really only one option, get better at dealing with fear. Learn to dance with it rather than resist it. Maybe that wild stallion can be trained into a world class racehorse and you, the jockey, are directing it towards the finish line as you work in synergy with each other. Let it energise you and not overrun you.

Let me give you an example to make it real. A few years ago, I took up jogging to get fit, lose weight, and just feel better. It was a real struggle at first, so I set myself a 90-day challenge to create a habit of running. This way I could feel that each run was an important contribution to the result I wanted to achieve. Honestly self-discipline mostly got me through, but I was starting to enjoy it more and more. I noticed that whilst I was running, I was also able to feel the fear that was held in my body. The first thing I noticed was my breathing would quicken and edge closer to hyperventilation. If I had to stop or slow down it was most often because I had lost control of my breathing rather than something else like my legs being tired. I noticed that beneath this fear was a very subtle calmness that when I would 'hang out with' it somehow allowed the fear to ease. I was fascinated by this and thought I'd keep the habit of running to experience this more.

So, I booked in my first marathon and intensified my training. At the start of my marathon run, I noticed my mind was judging if I should be ahead of someone or they should be ahead of me. It was exhausting and so quickly became clear to me that this was a pointless habit. So, I decided to look up at the overhanging branches as I ran to give my mind nothing to judge. It worked, my body relaxed, and my breathing calmed. I also started to combine this with hanging out in my feet and other areas of my body where tension was building. If I would just stay there with my awareness and just feel rather than think the tension would reduce. It was amazing! I really enjoyed my first marathon run and felt great even after the run.

I had to keep this going. So, what was next? What about 100km from London to Brighton, I thought? 2 marathons and then 10 miles on top of that! All in one day and only 6 months away! My mind was whirring with fear at the prospect of it and that was exactly why it was the right challenge for me. On the day of the run, I was more scared. I was absolutely committed to finishing. My mind just had no idea how. It was an epic experience and I needed to use all my focus to tame my mind. Especially when it started to play thoughts of wanting to be done. I just focused on hanging out in my body, noticing my breathing and the thoughts soon disappeared. 16 hours later I crossed the finish line, late into the evening. I was exhausted but I had discovered an energy inside of me that was far beyond what my mind thought I was capable of.

The reason I am telling you this because I want you to experience this same feeling; To find the powerful you that is full of energy is, in my experience, is a process of letting go. Letting go of the stories of the fixed mindset that are not absolutely true and being open to what is. My hope is that through your journey, you be open to a constantly developing you, the one with a growth mindset, an open heart and full of energy. An energy that was there all along, waiting for you to discover it.

I'm definitely still on my journey and learning to enjoy it more and more. I've shared my insights and system with many of my clients. I've helped them grow their mindsets so that they can feel more intensely alive with a powerful inner confidence and a deep knowing that they and what they have to offer matters.

If you are curious about what is possible for you or a loved one, then I have a special gift for you. If you send 'Energetic me' to hello@restoreyourbodynow.co.uk then I will send you a complimentary video series to get you started on your journey.

Tara Sutton

Unlocking the weight of loss

With 20 years' experience of working with clients dealing with grief and loss, Tara specialises in supporting women in their 40's who have made themselves busy in life to avoid dealing with the pain following the loss of a loved one.

Tara helps her clients to unlock and release painful memories allowing them to find peace with their passing. She equips them with the techniques and confidence to manage stressful situations with ease, allowing them to take back control over their emotional wellbeing.

Grief is a hugely taboo subject and Tara is on a mission to change this. She wants people to feel free to talk openly about those they have lost and include them on their journey through life.

Email: hello@tarasutton.co.uk for a complimentary 20 min discovery call

What They Don't Tell You When You Lose A Loved One...

So you might be thinking, quite rightly, what's that got to do with energy? Actually, in reality, it's got everything to do with energy. We ARE energy.

Connecting to those around us, family and friends, is extremely important for our wellbeing. When we shut ourselves off from society, this can have a huge impact not only on our emotional well-being but also on our physical and mental health. And one of the most impactful, heart wrenching and traumatic experiences we ever have to deal with is to lose someone we love.

In this chapter we will look at how those around us have an effect on our energy and my top three things to do to increase your energy and feel better connected to yourself.

If you are reading this and you have lost someone you deeply love and care for (and it doesn't matter how long ago that was!) then I send you all the love in the world and a huge hug and hope you have people in your life that you can turn to that support you wholeheartedly through it.

For most this won't be the case. Sadly we live in a society that thinks losing someone is something to eventually 'get over'. It's as if we are allowed the funeral to say our final goodbyes and then after a certain amount of allowed time has passed you are meant to be seen to get on with life pretty much as if nothing has happened!!! But how can you? You are a different person now to the person you were before and with a different life outlook!

It's at this point many of my clients turn to me for support as they are left completely drained and disconnected from life and they feel totally alone in their feelings.

I help them find connection in life again so they can take back control of their life and feel included once again and form a new relationship with the person they lost so that they can remember them with love.

Because the thing they don't tell you when you lose a loved one is that only our physical body dies. So there's no need for people to feel they only get that one chance to say goodbye. Remember I said earlier we are made of energy? Well, that is true after our physical body dies. Our energy continues to exist in the Universe!

It is often said that grief is love with nowhere to go – if we continue to connect with our loved ones by talking about them and to them then (and this is absolutely not pretending they are still alive!!) our love goes with that and it heals our grief little by little which in turns helps us to connect and support our own energy.

It's healthy to talk about them after they've gone. Something I experienced the absolute opposite of when I was a child and my father died. The effect it had on my health and life stayed with me for many years. There was a deep well of grief that I didn't deal with for 15 years until after my mother died and I was allowed to talk about him again.

It was a cold March morning when the doorbell rang. It was a lady who lived close to us and after inviting herself in for a chat she said in a rather matter of fact way – "I saw your mum leave early this morning in a rush – has your dad died yet?" And that is how I found out that my dad wasn't coming home from hospital in two weeks as my mother had reassured me only days before. I started asking questions and was abruptly told by a well-meaning member of the family to stop asking questions and go to my room as it was upsetting my mother. You see, my parents were very much in love and in my mother's own distraught realisation of losing her husband and all the other adults trying to protect her no one saw two little girls who had just lost their father needing love. So my twin and I went to our room as instructed and sat there in disbelief.

So that morning was more than the day my father died. It was the day that I realised that it turned out everyone else knew my father was dying, the day I was stopped asking questions, the day I stopped talking about my dad because it was too upsetting to everyone else to even mention his name. In those next 15 years I also made those into beliefs that I lived my life by - I'm not worthy of being included, everyone knows things that I don't, I don't have the right to have a voice to be heard. You can imagine how that impacted on my life; it wasn't good I can assure you!!

Do you have beliefs about you and your life from situations like this?! It's never too late to deal with them and I am glad to say I now have different beliefs to what happened that day and I beam a huge smile now whenever I think of my dad!

Try these tips to increase or sense your energy:

Rub your hands together then hold them in front you facing each other like you were holding a football. Then move them towards each other until you feel some resistance and you have just felt your energy!

Write a letter to a person you have lost. Write everything you've always wanted to say to them. Sit quietly, light a candle and read it out aloud. When we read something out loud rather than in our own heads it takes on a different energy, it goes out into the Universe and is extremely healing to our own bodies.

Go hug a tree – yep! A tree! Now this might sound a bit odd but it really works and will raise your energy immensely. (Please make sure you choose a tree that doesn't have poisonous leaves or berries!)

I firmly believe that we can form a new relationship with someone we've lost. We don't have to say our forever goodbye. We can form a new connection, take them with us on our journey through life so that we can openly 'Remember them With Love'. If you are curious to find out more, I am offering a discovery call with readers of this book. To book your 30 Minute complimentary call with me please email:

Tara Sutton

Email: hello@tarasutton.co.uk

Sarah Watt

Unlocking your potential through the power of movement

With over 5 years of experience in the fitness industry, working with clients all over the world, Sarah specialises in helping women in their 30s get off the vicious 'fast fix' diet rollercoaster and get on the 'self-development rocket' of sustainable results.

Through personalised workouts, easy-to-follow diet plans and motivational mindset coaching, Sarah helps her clients reconnect with their goals, enhance their self-confidence and unlock their potential through the power of movement. After just 6 months of working with Sarah, 60% of her clients go on to both achieve a promotion and lose a dress size. To Sarah, exercise is so much more than just weight loss, exercise is rocket fuel for the head and heart.

Website: www.sarahwattfitness.com

Email: info@sarahwattfitness.com

Instagram: @sarahwattfitness

Phone: +44(0)7595991185

What If I Told You That There Was Something You Could Do Right Now To Give You More Energy?

"Energy is like discovering your passion, listening to it, exploring it. It's a forward charging spirit."

(Ahrendts, 2013).

What if I told you that there was something you could do right now to give you more energy? Something that's free, guaranteed to get you results and only takes up 2% of your day?

Got the answer yet?

Yep, you got it. Exercise.

We've all heard about it, and I go into a bit more detail about the power of movement later, but surely that's not the only natural solution to feeling energised? What about in situations when going for a run or a walk just isn't an option?

Imagine this. It's a gorgeous sunny afternoon. You really enjoyed your 6am run, you've had such a productive morning, but now you're stuck in the office and can feel yourself drifting off. You've been in this meeting on 'Mitigating Change' for an hour already and it's not looking like it's going to finish anytime soon. You're looking for a natural energy boost, not another artificially sweet, or caffeinated one. Well, the good news is that I have a solution for you.

My name is Sarah Watt, and I help my clients to feel better, move better and be better by unlocking their potential through the power of movement. With over 5 years of experience in the health and fitness industry, I'm going to share with you my '5 Step Energiser Tool Kit' that I use with my clients to help them move better and feel better. These natural and easy to implement 'energizers', are designed to give you more energy, so you too can unlock your 'forward charging spirit'.

Despite living and breathing exercise every day, it hasn't always been that way. I hated exercise growing up. As a teenager I suffered with a real lack of self-confidence, felt embarrassed getting changed for P.E and would use every excuse to avoid Cross Country. It wasn't until I was diagnosed with an underlying heart condition at the age of 21, that everything changed. The summer before my final year of university I had to have open heart surgery, and following that, a year of rehab to rebuild my strength. It was through this rehabilitation programme that I started to learn about the powerful effects of movement. As my strength grew, so did my self-confidence, and after years of studying it inspired me to start my own award winning personal training company. Now I help women discover their potential through the power of movement, both inside and outside of the gym.

Take one of my clients Jane for example. We started working together about 9 months ago, and at the time, she wanted to lose weight and get more energy. She lacked self-confidence, was always fatigued and felt uncomfortable in her own skin. Despite getting enough sleep, she woke up feeling tired, and didn't do much at the weekend because she was exhausted from work. Fast forward to now, Jane has dropped 2 dress sizes, ran her first ever 5k and qualified in a new profession which got her promoted. After just 9 months of working together, and implementing my energizer tools, Jane has truly stepped up both in her personal and professional life. In her own words, she's got her "mojo back".

So how do you get your mojo back?

This is where my '5 Step Energiser Tool Kit' comes in.

1. **Scheduled Activity** - I may be biased but this is by far the most influential thing you can do to help you feel more energised. Exercise is a natural stress reducer, mood booster and sleep enhancer. Just 30 minutes a day has shown to improve your energy, focus and cardiovascular health. During and after exercise our bodies pump a greater amount of oxygenated blood, glucose and 'feel good' neurotransmitters around the body giving you that natural boost.

   TIP Aerobic exercise (e.g. running, walking, swimming) vs anaerobic exercise (e.g. heavy weight training) is more effective at generating long lasting energy. Anaerobic training produces more lactic acid and is more taxing on the central nervous system, so requires greater recovery time. So if you want more energy, schedule exercise first thing in the morning, and opt for aerobic.

2. **Stay Hydrated** - ideally with filtered water, and keep caffeinated drinks to a minimum; they will ironically dehydrate you. Lemons and limes are a healthy and tasty addition, and may encourage you to drink more. Keep a bottle or glass in every

room to help form a memory cue and get into good habits of staying hydrated.

TIP too often we only drink when we're thirsty. To keep your brain and body operating as its best, drink even when you don't feel thirsty, and avoid feeling dehydrated.

3. Slow Breathing - like breathing, energy is something that you can both take in (inhale) and give away (exhale), so let's maximise your ability to breathe! Breathing in through the nose, straight to the diaphragm, is so much more effective at getting oxygen into the lungs compared to gasping for air through the mouth.

TIP the next time you start yawning or feel yourself drifting off in that meeting at work, try taking 5 deep breaths (3 seconds in and 3 seconds out) through the nose and see how awesome you feel. Our body loves oxygen, so get diaphragmatic breathing!

4. Sleeping Power - Are you getting 7-9 hours a night but still waking up feeling tired? Perhaps it's not the quantity, but more the quality of your sleep. We all know it's important, it's vital for maintaining your physical and mental health. If you aren't making sleep a priority in your life already, I strongly recommend you do.

TIP try wearing an eye mask to bed, or opening a window. Sometimes our environments interfere with our sleep, reducing its quality. Also try getting up and going to bed at the same time every day, a structured body clock could be your answer.

5. Super Food - we've all been tempted to reach

for the sugary snacks when we start to feel tired, but that's often the worst thing you could do. As it causes a spike in your insulin and blood sugar levels, to then just drop further down the line. So think about keeping sugar to a minimum and avoid having it first thing in the morning or last thing at night. Ensure you have a good source of protein, 2 to 3 vegetables and complex carbohydrates with every meal to help better balance your energy throughout the day. More details are outlined in my monthly recipe eBooks.

TIP avoid having cereal for breakfast; anything high in both carbohydrates and sugar will cause that spike and leave you craving more sweet things throughout the day. This will also leave you feeling more lethargic and more likely to overeat. So when you fancy a snack, reach for filtered water, nuts, or berries to keep you going.

*** BONUS TOOL ***

This is the one thing that most people leave out, but it is the one thing that ensures every other step works in the long term.

Stay Accountable - let me guess, in the past you've had every intention of maintaining those healthy habits, but they've never lasted? When it comes to creating a habit, consistency and enjoyment is key, and that's what I work on with my clients to get them results. To find out more, book in your free 20 minute coaching session with me now. Details below.

TIP Get a journal. Every morning write down your energy boosting intentions for the day, and at the end of the day, write down what you have achieved. How did you feel? What could you do differently? If that isn't enough, get an accountability buddy, and check in with them to help ground those habits into the subconscious.

There is so much more I wish I could share with you. If you would like to find out more about how I can help you get your 'mojo' back, then let's chat! As you're reading this book, I'd love to gift you a copy of the journal I use with my clients, a copy of one of my awesome recipe eBooks and a free 20 minute coaching session with me to help get you into action and start feeling more energised. Simply send me an email titled 'MOJO' to info@sarahwattfitness.com and let's ignite your 'forward charging spirit' now.

Bonus Chapter

Emotion Creates Motion = Energy

Enthusiasm is the glue that holds everything together. With anything you want to accomplish or do in life, if you have enthusiasm and energy it makes you more likely to succeed. It will also more likely attract others who want to help your success because enthusiasm is contagious.

Enthusiasm empowers us to take action, to keep going no matter what the obstacle and perhaps, most importantly, to make decisions. Did you know that the first step to making a decision is emotion?

That's right. Emotion creates motion = Energy!

Think about the last time you made a big decision. I bet something moved your emotions enough to get you to take action. The reality is, we make decisions emotionally and then justify them logically. It isn't logic that gets us to decide what we want – it's our emotions. The logic might build the case for making one decision over another. However, it is our emotions that step us over from indecision to deciding. Our logical brain is used before and after the act of deciding but the actual decision itself is all emotional.

One of the greatest emotions that leads to action is enthusiasm. As a matter of irrefutable fact, your level of enthusiasm has greater influence on anyones willingness to purchase anything from you, partner with you, or generally do anything with you compared to the influence of your title, qualifications or any other logical piece of information about you.

Which means, the more energy and enthusiasm you can bring to everything you do, the more likely you are to succeed and the more likely you are to attract other people to come on the journey with you.

Ever hear the saying „attitude determines altitude"?

This is very true.

Your personal attitude greatly influences your results. Imagine meeting with someone just after you got into a minor car accident that wasn't your fault. How would your attitude be? Would you walk into that meeting a little „off –mood?" Probably yes! And of course, this is going to hurt your chances of that meeting going well.

You see, no matter what your attitude, you must learn to manage it so it reflects the energy and enthusiasm necessary for completing and succeeding whatever it is what you're doing. Fundamentally, people don't want to associate with someone who has low enthusiasm and poor attitude and this is true in life as well as business. Whether your significant-other just ended your relationship, or you just got a speeding ticket, check your energy level and your attitude at the door before doing anything where the outcome matters to you.

To do this, simply take a minute or two and give yourself a pep talk out loud. Or, if you have more time, find an empty office or room, close the door behind you, and repeat the following phrase out loud:

„ I'm a winner. I create success no matter what. And I'm the best!"

Repeat this phrase until you have convinced yourself

that you are a winner and no matter what happens you will create success, then put a smile on your face and walk outside. There is nothing more powerful and energetic than greeting a client or entering a meeting with a smile gently fading off your face.

You may think this is corny or silly, but that's exactly why it works. There is no way you can't laugh or smile if you do this. Just remember to have the door closed behind you so others don't think you're a nut while you do it!

This exact technique has produced thousands of dollars in additional revenue for me because I took the time to get my head right before meeting potential clients.

When I first learned this technique from Brian Tracy, I thought it was a silly joke. In fact I thought it was so silly I failed to use it for many months until one day I had such a bad day that I said. „What the heck... it can't hurt."

And you know what? It didn't.

After I gave myself a pep talk, I felt so silly and goofy that I started laughing at myself. As I walked out to greet my potential new client with that smile on my face, I immediately found that they began to smile as well. Why? Because smiling and laughter are contagious and it = Energy !

The outcome of that presentation was $9,000

Not a bad result for having a bad day, huh ☺ ?

So here is the deal...bring your highest energy and enthusiasm to everything you do and you'll be amazed at how it is reflected back at you from everyone you meet so you become even more energized and enthusiastic. This positive spiral will create better and better results in your life, job or business and very soon, high energy will be your habitual way of approaching everything.

Now, you‘ve read about my experience and I now wanna read yours!

And I know you’re going to top my levels of success because by now, your energy and enthusiasm is going to be unstoppable. If you maintain this high energy and enthusiasm in everything you do, success isn’t just likely, it’s inevitable! So, send me an email and let me know about the outstanding life you’re creating for yourself simply by stepping up your energy in everything you do!

Wishing you every success!

David

David Gil Cristobal

website: www.davidgilcristobal.com

Eamil: david@davidgilcristobal.com

Phone: +41(0)79 311 04 61

David is a multi-bestselling author and considered Switzerland’s leading Success and Wealth Mentor. Living in Basel with his wife Lea, David has spent more than 20 years helping others reach their highest levels of success. His products, events, coaching programs, and mentorship is designed to help you achieve more than you ever thought possible in less time.

Congratulations!

Now you've reached the end of the book, the action starts. Depending on how you have read this book, now might be the time to go back and take some notes or even re-read a couple of chapters.

What are your key learnings from what you've read?

What are the top 5 things that you can perhaps change, tweak or add into your life to make a difference based on what you have read? Take the time to write these down as the act of writing will help cement them in your mind.

1.

2.

3.

4.

5.

Reading is of course valuable, yet it's taking action on what we've learned that creates change in our lives. Change can be both scary and exciting because it means doing things differently and creating a different and perhaps unknown outcome. With what you've learned from this book and the actions you're now going to take, what might now be possible for you, your family or loved ones?

Often, we look at the negatives of change and keep ourselves stuck because it feels safer.

We would challenge you to look at the positives of change and get yourself moving physically or metaphorically. List out 5 great things that might be possible for you if you started adopting some of the suggestions from this book:

1.

2.

3.

4.

5.

By the way, if you found it challenging fill in this list, perhaps going back and re-reading or studying some of the chapters could help you get clear on what could become possible for you now.

However, if you're struggling with the idea of re-reading a book or 'studying' it then perhaps this example might help. As a Bikram yoga devotee, Karene used to do the same 26 postures in every Bikram yoga class and she used to do 1 or 2 classes every day. Yet every time, each class was different because she was different. Perhaps she had slept differently, or had different experiences meaning she had more or less energy to bring to class. Some days her favourite posture turned out to be the one she struggled with the most; or the one posture she didn't usually like became the one that made a real difference to her mood that day! It is same with books....there is always something new to 'see' when we re-read something because each time we read it, we are different. We have a different mindset and different emotions because we've had different experiences since we last read the book.

This means we are going to notice and remember different things when we re-read it.

So, by all means if you have enjoyed this book, pass it on to a friend, colleague or loved one and also revisit and re-read it for the lessons, stories and possibilities it might provide for you in the future. We know that not all of the authors, stories or experiences will resonate with you first time round and yet others may be the start of a new journey for you. We encourage you to reach out personally to those authors who 'spoke' to you to see what else they might be able to offer as support on your journey or just to feed back the difference their words have made for you.

We all go through life as individuals, however, it is the experience of relating to other humans where the magic happens. When we relate to others, we learn more about ourselves. We hope that this book has allowed you to 'meet' some more people and gain a deeper understanding of yourself.

We, and the authors who have made this possible, wish you every success with your journey.

Best wishes

Chris, Karene & David

About The Authors & Hcb Publishing

David Gil Cristobal turns people into brands so they earn what they are worth and conquer the box seat in their customer's head. With more than three decades experience in the sports arena, David had a long career as a professional soccer player, before co-founding Eerion Performance, one of Switzerland's top health and fitness organisations, and launching Fitness Fortune University where he turns health and fitness professionals into elite fitness businesses in as little as 90 days.

Armed with a masters degree in business management and leadership and his own stellar business success, David speaks 6 languages, has presented to more than 10,000 people from 30+ companies in 10 different countries, is a best-selling author with 5 books in 2 different languages and has starred in a motion picture.

Chris and Karene Lambert-Gorwyn are the founders of Heart Centred Business Ltd and the authors of the #1 Amazon Best-Selling Book, Grow Your Heart Centred Business from Passion to Profit. Having built multiple 5, 6 and 7 figure businesses of their own, Chris & Karene have been humbled with numerous Business Awards. They've spoken at Business and Financial conferences around the world in 14 different countries on 4 different continents, meeting business titans such as Sir Richard Branson, Les Brown, Tony Robbins, Randi Zuckerberg, Kevin Harrington, Gill Fielding, Nick James, Kane & Alessia Minkus and Robert & Kim Kiyosaki.

Chris & Karene grow Heart Centred Businesses and their clients typically increase their income by £50,000-100,000 within 12 months of implementing their systems. Teaching the right things in the right order, Chris & Karene have personally trained more than 3000 practitioners and experts how to build 6 figure businesses.

HCB Publishing

Chris, Karene and David founded HCB Publishing to help more business owners share their expertise with the world Do you have a special skill or expertise? Would you be curious to know how to use books to exponentially grow your business?

If you want to talk further and get direct support from Chris, Karene and David to take your business and income to a totally different level, register on the link below and explore how you might be able to achieve your dreams much quicker than you thought by working together.

As successful business owners, we've coached and trained thousands of clients to success.

We're fortunate to make our living doing what we love, which is helping other experts to become successful.

But, it wasn't always easy. We all started out like most authors with no platform, no database, no experience, and a whole lot of questions. We spent many years figuring out how to sell books from scratch, build businesses, learn what works, and what doesn't. But you don't have to learn the hard way like we did. We're here to share with you what works and what doesn't so you can write and sell your expertise via books and increase your reputation and your income.

Take the next step in your Author Career and work with us directly. Click on the link below for more details about your next steps:

www.hcbpublishing.com

Work with us and learn how to use books to grow your

income and your business!

Printed in Great Britain
by Amazon

57145385R00078